INDOCTRINATION
IMPEDES
MIND MATURATION

2nd Edition

INDOCTRINATION IMPEDES MIND MATURATION

2nd Edition

Romeo Gauvreau, B.A.,

ARPress
ILLUMINATING IDEAS.
EMPOWERING VOICES

ARPress
45 Dan Road Suite 5
Canton MA 02021
Hotline: 1(888) 821-0229
Fax: 1(508) 545-7580

Ordering Information:

Quantity sales. Special discounts are available on quantity purchases by corporations, associations, and others. For details, contact the publisher at the address above.

Printed in the United States of America.

ISBN-13:   Paperback   979-8-89356-030-5
                  eBook   979-8-89356-031-2

Library of Congress Control Number: 2024902954

Table Of Contents

Special Thanks

First, I dedicate this book

To my mother, Mélanie Caron Gauvreau, Whose insight and courage,

In the face of a life of subjugation, Have inspired me with this book writing.

To my elementary school teacher, Miss Estelle Landry

Who has taught me how to read and write, to my students and to all the students at the school of life.

To my children, François, Bernard and Annie, To Judy's children, Grant and Craig.

To my granddaughter, Charlotte Nicole, and

To this woman who has witnessed my descent in hell too many times, and has received me with open arms

On my way back, my wife Judy.

Preface

Like through a long pregnancy, I have been carrying this book in my heart and soul since 1968-69. I'm not qualified to write this book. I mean I'm not a university professor, **a** psychologist or a sociologist. I have been involved with the school system for close to 17 years as a student and for 6 years as a teacher.

To me, it was long enough to find out that I didn't like school after grade 5 and that I loved my 6 years of teaching in spite of the fact that I disliked the school system. Through those 6 years, I refused to do what I considered harmful to the students… and I got away with it.

I quit after my sixth year in spite of the generous offer from my principal. He offered me a position as one of his assistants with double the salary. I turned him down and quit teaching altogether. I could not stand the school board's politics…or the coercive atmosphere of the school.

To all of you dear readers who have accepted my invitation to share a few ideas and reflections through the pages that will follow, I say a heartfelt thank you. In the same manner as we're not a stand-up comedian without an audience, we're not an author without the reader. I need you to receive me; I need to confide in you and to share all these thoughts that weigh me down.

Introduction

Although the word indoctrination is well known, its real implications might not be clear or of interest to most people. There is a hidden depth to this concept, a depth that most people don't suspect or care about. One of the reasons why most are not aware of its profound effect on them is because they are like deers mesmerized by the headlights of a car; they are rendered blind to its existence and its hypnotizing effects on them.

The agents of indoctrination are like surgeons doing an operation. They administer a strong dose of anesthetics so that the patient doesn't feel what is being done to him/her. The anesthetic of choice for the indoctrination operators is to put the mind of unsuspecting people to sleep with promises of rewards in this world or in the other,...or both. It's also the coaxing into believing falseness and fairy tales that change the perceived reality of life, making it full of magic and of false hope.

The best example that comes to mind is to convince people that if they pray to God and ask Him, He will change the course of reality for them by removing the consequences of certain of their actions, which consequences they have attracted to themselves by acting against nature. It's like to make a kid believe that he can throw as many rocks in the air as he wants to, and if he prays God to protect him, the rocks will not hit him on the head when they come back down to earth. *"You'd better get a helmet, kid!" If one of these rocks is perpendicularly above your head when it comes down, God or no God, you're going to learn about the law of gravity... and fast!*

Before I go any further with my babbling, let me make something clear. Please do not believe a word you're going to read in this book. This book might contain some truth. This book is void of knowledge. Instead, it contains beliefs. Mine and whatever remnant of the indoctrination imposed on me by my parents, my teachers, the catholic church, the government, the consumerism shenanigans, the media, and many other sources including my own auto-brainwashing.

Yes, we do brainwash ourselves. We have been violated from a young age with constant brainwashing and we became like mental masochists and ended up brainwashing ourselves to some extent. An example of it is what we do to ourselves when we look in the mirror and tell ourselves that we're not attractive enough and therefore our self-worth is diminished. And that, in spite of the fact that we might be attractive and that our parents and everybody else tell us we are so.

I have a *PhD. in B.S...* I'm warning you. What you're reading is not the truth. It is MY truth and hopefully the truth about me. Instead, hear me and if by any chance some of my beliefs pass the scrutiny of your *"built-in bullshit detector"*, you can choose to believe or to flush them down the drain of your indifference.

This book is about how pernicious indoctrination of any kind is. The word doctrine has a religious connotation but is not restricted to religions' doctrines. Family upbringing is most of the time a carrier of indoctrination of religious and cultural origin. The school system partners with the family and the church in using indoctrination in order to achieve its goals: get all students to obey no matter what, to believe a ton of historical and religious falsenesses, to submit to their quasi military discipline and get a grade 12 diploma.

But I will get back to the subject of our *"famous"* school system and its hidden agenda. For the moment, let's have a close look at what indoctrination is, after having read this poem I wrote a few years ago. I hope you'll enjoy it and let it touch you.

Say brother, say sister

Will you help me
When we meet on the often dusty roads of life
Please will you help me through the maze that those dusty
roads often form?
Through the endless paths with the ill illuminated cul-de-sacs,
Where I roam too often aimlessly,
Between those high walls offering slits of skies but no
exits?
Those high walls who, too often,
talk of hopelessness, fear and despair?

Say brother, say sister

Will you help me shift my sight from those walls of resistance
Towards those slits of sky full of light and promises?
Will you show me how to decorate those walls
With arrangements of pebbles of colour
Using the mud from the path as cement to
Form many flowers of many petals?

Say brother, say sister

Will you help me draw on these walls,
Straighter paths with happy destinations?
And thus help me enjoy the journey?
Remind me that happiness is not a destination,
But a way of travelling
A journey made of moments pregnant
of anticipation and discovery?

Romeo Gauvreau, B.A.,

Say brother, say sister

Will you help me shift my sight from your tired body
To those slits in your face, to the smile on your lips,
To the twinkle in your eyes?
These portals of your heart, these doors to your soul,
Inviting me to a sweet rocking?
In that refuge full of hospitality,
Help me find myself, help me find my way?
Let me see your uniqueness,
Your Source energy, your divine ancestry.
Let me see the light reflecting from every fiber
of your spiritual being.
Let me reflect in these mirrors of your soul
that are your mysterious eyes.
And doing so,
Let me realize how much we're alike,
in beauty, in grandeur,
in heart hospitality.

Say brother, say sister

Will you help me see all that in you, in me, in all that is?
If you do that for you, for me, for others,
You will be the best teacher,
of light, of life, of possibilities,
of happiness eternal;
of Love.

Say brothers, say sisters, I Love you, all of You.
Roméo Gauvreau, poem composed and delivered at a
poetry slam Café in Bali, Indonesia, May 20, 2006

CHAPTER 1

Indoctrination: what is it?

"The sad truth about humanity...is that people believe what they're told. Maybe not the first time, but by the hundredth time, the craziest of ideas just becomes a given."

— Neal Shusterman, UnWholly

At first glance, indoctrination implies the transmission of doctrines, beliefs, theories etc. to a chosen group of people or to the masses. Most of the times, when we talk of doctrines, we're talking about religions' teachings. The word indoctrination is not limited to religious doctrines. In fact, indoctrination bombards us from a very young age till our death. It teaches us to accept a set of beliefs without questioning them.

It's an attempt at imposing beliefs, theories, advices, instructions, propaganda and numerous other forms of imposition of instructions on our minds by parents, teachers, churches, and governments, to name a few. Most of the time we're not aware of being mentally bombarded by people who want *"what's best for us"*. Kids start very young to protest and rebel against it.

By the time they enter school, they have been trained to accept -or resign themselves to- that invasion of their soul, but they have no choice but to submit to the school system and its coercive *modus operandi*. At the same time, in lots of cases, they have also been dragged to church by parents' persuasion and coaxing. Depending on the church, the kids will dislike this manipulation at various degrees, without having the choice to refuse to go. The use of seduction under the form of promises of going to heaven and other fairy tales succeed to convince many of them to resign themselves to that despicable drudgery.

Indoctrination is brainwashing imposed on people under the pretext that it's for the glory of God and their own good. Every means are good to reach the goal of the indoctrinator, which goal is never for the benefit of its victims. In the case of certain religions, it procures power, adulation, prestige and money, lots of money in certain cases, to the hierarchy of those churches.

If we look at the school system, it's not as easy to see the presence of indoctrination. School teaches to write, read and count first and then a variety of subjects supposedly giving knowledge to our kids. No indoctrination there… or could there be? Both the parents and the teachers tell the kids that they must go to school if they want to succeed in life and be happy. If they drop school, they're told that they will never get a job. In other words, they'll be bums and druggies at the expense of society and bla, bla, bla.

School also teaches a lot of things other than knowledge. One of the worse things it teaches them *is to obey.* There's nothing wrong, at first glance, in being taught to obey. They have no choice but to obey while in school. To obey every teacher and member of the staff, whatever they want, even if one thinks they're wrong, even if they *know* they're wrong.

Of course it's an advantage when we have to obey the laws in society. What would happen if people didn't stop at red lights? Everybody can easily agree with that last example. We know not to steal and there's a law in place to punish those who do. Those are all easy to understand examples. Let's complicate the problem a bit and look at the obedience the government expects from us, its citizens.

Is it always wise to obey the government blindly? If you believe the government is wrong in a particular circumstance, should you obey its demands? Or should you follow your inner voice and refuse to obey. Of course there will be consequences if you refuse to submit to a law you consider against the best interest of the people. There will be penalties, fines or even jail. If you value your integrity more than the risk of penalties, you will have to decide what's more important to you. Blind obedience is a form of subjugation learned at home, at school, at church and in society with its different institutions.

Another thing school teaches, is that you cannot trust adults. Adults lie when it suits them. The promise of success and happiness after a grade 12 education is a lie. Lots of students know it's a lie. And we should worry about those who don't.

The teachers pretend they care about all the students and that they teach and discipline them because they love them. Another lie! Some love students, but for the majority, it's a job, *only an underpaid job.* What they call discipline, in a lot of cases, is bullying. Most teachers bully students! Surprised? The school system functions by the use of a magic tool: coercion.

Coercion comes under the form of threats, mental abuse and punishment. That's the only way most teachers know how to keep their classes under control. They believe that without coercion, it would be total chaos. They're wrong! School can work without any coercion and produce much better results.

William Glasser, an American psychiatrist, has developed a school system that does just that: it uses no coercion. He calls it Quality School. There are some in the U.S. and in many European countries and even in Canada. There are not very many yet, since it only started around 25-30 years ago and it takes several years to convert a coercion driven school into a non-coercive school.

The biggest obstacle to the conversion is not the students. It's the teachers, in general, who do not want to let go of their sacred whip: the coercion. They're scared to lose control of their classes. You can read about it in his book: *The Quality School, Managing Students without Coercion.* Among other things students learn in school, we find deception, cheating, bullying, and prostitution of self.

Origins of indoctrination

I have no idea when it started. My guess is that it started when we were still more monkey than human. The first doctrines to appear on earth must have been about fear and how to protect ourselves from the elements and the gods' wrath. The thunder was probably seen as the gods being unhappy about us and groaning loudly, warning us to behave or else... The leaders, seeing the potential of these beliefs of their people started using that doctrine on their primitive fellowmen. They were feeling empowered by those manoeuvres. It gave them some prestige and respect. Manipulation had just been discovered. Brainwashing was born. Its limitless power had just been recognized and harnessed by society's leaders.

Later, it got adopted by parents, by the school systems, the governments, the justice systems, and many others including you and me, brothers.

When we say that somebody is good at convincing others, what are we really saying? Could we be using the wrong word? Shouldn't we be saying that he is good at manipulating others? Am I in the process of trying to convince you of some of my beliefs? Am I attempting to manipulate you?

Modus operandi

There is a part of the m.o. that is clear and evident to all. You sit in a church for 45 minutes. One person in the front is talking and nobody else is allowed to talk. Also, there are no Qs and As after the sermon...*or monologue.* The content, most of the time, tries to sway you in one direction chosen by the speaker. Every time, the same concepts gets repeated and hammered in your head. You're being brainwashed, manipulated, without being aware of the alienation taking place slowly but surely in your psyche; and that, with your consent, at some level. You're selling yourself short. You're distancing your apparent self from your true self.

This time you're sitting in class and the teacher is constantly reminding you, by his attitude, that he is the boss, that he knows everything and that, metaphorically, he has power of life or death over you. He can send you to the principal, throw you out of his class, have you suspended from school, flunk you, and the list continues. He expects total obedience to any and every whim of his, and, in lots of countries, he can resort to corporal punishments with the approval of the parents.

In the confines of the class, for all practical purposes, he is God! Our kids are at the total mercy of a person, the teacher, who may or may not be benevolent. Who may or may not like teaching and students. Who may or may not be honest, fair, mentally healthy, and apt at helping kids connect with themselves and others. And, consequently, to love themselves, others, and the whole creation around them. If he doesn't help them find themselves, discover who they really are, he can't help them find anything else of value, knowledge of any kind included. ***If we don't know self, we know nothing.*** Knowledge is only relevant if it connects you with yourself. Anything else is but instructions.

There is a very strong snobbery about knowledge, especially scientific knowledge. Knowledge has been made into a god by the people who have some or believe they have some. *A priori,* I do not necessarily consider knowledgeable a university teacher. Such a person has channelled 90% of his brain towards 1% of the knowledge available to him. He is mentally handicapped by his own choice. When such a person thinks about himself, he values himself first as an expert in a certain domain and second as a human being. He has funnelled his knowledge into a very narrow field. A small part of his brain works a lot, while the majority of his brain is idle and rusting away. That theory applies to most university teachers and professionals. They have prisms for glasses and see life through a distorted vision caused by their specialization.

All these knowledgeable people hearing me would laugh and tell you it's ludicrous and untrue. They would be mostly right. It is not the truth. It's only a concept I hold as the truth according to my point of view, from my perspective, my angle, my bias, and, ultimately, who I am. In that sense, it's only *MY* truth, and maybe, a small part of *THE* truth.

Different Contents

The content of indoctrination is as varied as the number of manipulators at work. They all have a doctrine, a story, a sales pitch, a seductive proposition, a favor they need, especially your money or... your body etc. For them, it's as imperative to convince you, as it is for the drug addict to get his next fix.

Its aims

The aim or avowed goal of the indoctrinator is always to help you feel more secure, to enjoy more comfort, to be happier, to have more money, to become a better person, to go to heaven etc. The real goal of the indoctrinator is a different story. He's seeking power, control, adulation, fame, prestige, MONEY, and a myriad of other personal benefits.

When somebody extorts money from somebody else, I'm not sure that the gain of money is what pleases him most. I believe that it's probably the process of fooling you that tickles him more than the money itself. Because money, he might have a lot of and not really needing more. To a con, the conning itself makes him feel superior to you, and ...maybe to everybody else. He feels powerful and smarter than everybody else and that is, for him, a fix comparable or superior to crack cocaine. That's possibly his way of compensating for his low self-esteem and the hatred of who he is.

True nature of indoctrination

The true nature of indoctrination is manipulation of your psyche in order to replace an important part of its content with a specific content chosen carefully to coax you into accepting as truth: fairy tales, lies, deception. It's an insidious machination that provokes confusion and alienation. It's systematic brainwashing which will interfere with your mental and spiritual development. You're not yourself anymore; you're a twisted version of your authentic self.

End results of indoctrination:

The first and the most important end result of indoctrination is a strong impediment to self-discovery and self-actualization and in definitive, self love. It's also a strong impediment to civilization, as we call it. I will, if you don't mind, substitute the word civilization with humanization. We can have civilization without humanization, but not the other way around.

This alienation at a global level provokes isolation and a division of individuals, of people and of countries. It also provokes a certain disconnecting between individuals, ending up in a social discomfort and a certain uneasiness. In a word, it becomes a social *dis-ease*. We often hear in French: *"Le monde est malade!"* or in plain English: *"the world is sick!"*

What can we do?

Before anything else, we must gradually realize the widespread presence of indoctrination in society. We can't solve a problem that we don't first acknowledge having. The next step is to identify where the problem has its roots.

Everything we see in society starts in the family. We must educate ourselves to try and stop brainwashing our kids at home.

If the school would replace most of the insipid curriculum with education of our children in subjects pertinent to their life, like how to establish and maintain healthy relationships with self and others, using the two magic ingredients: love and respect, it would be a giant step towards real education. How to deal with the opposite sex, *how not to get pregnant*, for girls, how to succeed in marriage, why not to use coercion when raising kids etc. Those are a sample of practical and very important subjects.

In order to make possible the teaching of these subjects, you have to educate the parents -those who are still salvageable- until a majority accepts that you teach *these taboo subjects* to their kids. This alone would take at least 5 to 7 years if they collaborate. That's in populations that don't have an extreme culture. What do I call an extreme culture? For me, for example, a culture where we still find arranged marriage or the practice of FGM, or Feminine Genital Mutilation, are extremes cultures.

Marriage is a very important relationship most of us embrace in early life. Let's say you take a man wanting to get married and give him the option to choose among ten beautiful and well-educated women. By well educated, I mean raised the right way. If we agree that he has also been raised the right way, not indoctrinated nor alienated –if it exists- he will still have to get to know them personally before he chooses which one suits his personality and his taste better. In a word, which one is most compatible with him.

The fact that all ten women are perfect doesn't mean that they're all perfect for him. Nobody can, or should choose for him. The consequences of a mismatched marriage are very severes for the spouses, but often irreparables and destructives for the children who are victims of it.

After we've lowered the indoctrination level at home, we must try to do the same at school. It would be nice if we could do it in that order, but I think the family and the school indoctrination intermingle with each other. They must be tackled simultaneously. Knowing how long it takes to implement a Quality School, we have to count at least a few years for a basic *"des-indoctrination"*. When we talk about teaching proper sex education in school, we must count even longer. Ideally, it should be mostly done at home by the parents.

Indoctrination at church is even more difficult to deal with, because of the amount of brainwashing involved for the last millennia. Fear is a strong weapon used for the control of people and most religions use fear to keep their flock in line. Fear of God is pretty well as scary a weapon as it gets. However, these changes will *usually* not happen in one generation. The coming generation will_possibly make a big step forward, compared with previous generations. It's only speculation on my part. It's too early to say, but there are some signs of disconnect with the old ways…

Finally, let's help kids *develop a built-in bullshit detector at the entrance of their mind*. They shouldn't believe anything coming from outside of themselves, unless and until, they decide that it's helpful for them to believe it.

CHAPTER 2

Tools or agents of indoctrination:

''Tell people there's an invisible man in the sky who created the universe, and the vast majority believe you. Tell them the paint is wet, and they have to touch it to be sure.''

— George Carlin

Religions

The first agent that comes to mind is religion. Most people are born in a family practicing a certain religion. It's less true now than when I was young, but in some countries, close to 100% of children gets born from parents who will force their religious beliefs on their kids. It's an integral part of their culture and they believe it's for the good of their children. They are ready to disown their kid if he refuses to practice the parent's religion. Those are extremes, of course, but it shows how strong cultural brainwashing can be. In the less extreme cases, parents just brainwashed their kids' minds, bribe them, threaten them and, in a word, coerce them into behaving the way they want them to.

Religious indoctrination is the most pervasive of all since it deals with the spiritual journey of the individual. And it starts marking the child before he's born, through the mother's beliefs and behaviour. And it will influence his life in a very profound manner, even if, when he becomes an adult, he drops that religion. It's very difficult to erase the scars of such a devastating alienation. I abandoned the catholic religion in 1962-63 and I still experience its after effects.

School

The present school system in America was concocted and put in place by the Americans around 1855. Going to school is compulsory from age 6 to age 16. The avowed goal of the American government was to create a population of people easy to govern by using the process of conformism. Make everybody the same and teach them to obey no matter what. And if they all think the same way, it would be easy to govern and there wouldn't be any problem to enlist the youth in an army to go and kill strangers. Just ask and you got it! They already received a military discipline in school. It also aimed to prepare workers for the industry which is acceptable, to some extent. The bossing at work is counterproductive and poisons the workers' life.

In order to achieve their goal, they used the militia to force parents to send and keep their kids in school, under the threat of incarceration, which they used when needed. Canada introduced the compulsory public school system at the turn of the 20th century. It didn't take long for the religions to use the schools to propagate their doctrines by imposing their teaching of religion in class and the advertizing of their religion with crosses on the classroom walls. Also, prayers were made part of the curriculum.

Most Families

The majority of families being religious, the kids were raised in the religion of their parents and taught all kind of unbelievable fairy tales they had to believe -or pretend to believe- if they didn't want to be severely reprimanded. In the case of the catholic religion, they were introduced to a mean vengeful god threatening to throw them into hell if they dare touch their genitals, of all things.

The bible was telling them that the fear of God is the beginning of wisdom! But at the same time, teaching them that God is infinite love.

Why should you fear the most loving being in the universe who, they said, loves you unconditionally? That Supreme Being, they were told, is their father and creator!

Governments

The governments and the church were in cahoots to impose the teaching of religion at home and in school because brainwashed and ''conformised" kids were easier to control in society. School was teaching them to obey no matter what, no matter who. You tell them jump and they say: *"how high?"* kind of thing. Subjugated and enslaved people don't say *"No!"* to the government's demands. The administration of the country becomes easier and peaceful. Protestations and revolutions become unlikely.

Media

More and more, the media have a formidable influence on people. We get bombarded continuously by censured news, product advertizing and political propaganda.

News occupies a large place in the media through TV and radio mainly. The news we listen to, is not always the report of what really happened. Lots of countries censure the news to control and manipulate you.

Propaganda

They also pepper the news with propaganda aiming at presenting their country from a more favorable angle. They want to look their best and be respected *...or feared*. The propaganda part is brainwashing in its purest form. The masses must be kept alienated and passive. They must feel enough anxiety to continue consuming the market products. As long as they keep shopping, they keep working and the country's economy is remaining healthy. Also, when the drug of consumerism holds you in its grip, you don't plan protestations or revolutions.

Self

To list self as an agent of indoctrination seems surprising, to say the least. When you become an adult, after having been forced to believe incredible religious fairy tales for years, making yourself believe what you can't possibly believe, you learn to lie to yourself. Lying to others is not recommended. It's using deception and manipulation of somebody. But lying to yourself is the most dangerous practice one can do to ruin one's chance of finding who you really are. And when you lie to yourself, you are brainwashing and confusing yourself.

Auto-suggestion based on fear and ignorance aims at calming and reassuring yourself, but it can only lead to alienation. It's a type of prostitution, far more damageable than sexual prostitution. It's the worst betrayal you could ever bring onto yourself. Your chance at happiness, from then on, is extremely compromised.

CHAPTER 3

End results of indoctrination

"There are very few people who are going to look into the mirror and say, 'That person I see is a savage monster;' instead, they make up some construction that justifies what they do. "

— Noam Chomsky

Impediment to self-actualization, to civilisation and humanization is one of the end results of indoctrination. And it's the most serious consequence of that deplorable monstrosity. I believe that as long as there will be for religions the freedom and the permission to indoctrinate, there will never be real humanization. It's a serious accusation towards such religions and I'm aware of it.

How can it be an impediment to self actualisation? I believe strongly that the value of academic knowledge is exaggerated. Of course, the three Rs are an essential basic training.

After the student possesses those basic skills, the sky is the limit. He can, by himself, learn whatever he's curious about and interested in. And he can achieve that, school or no school, like in the case of un-schooling. Not many parents do it, but it's easier than home-schooling since there's no curriculum to follow or tests to pass.

Intelligence is not all it's said to be.

There's a tendency in society, to evaluate people by their level of intelligence and admire and respect them based on that. They judge that level of intelligence, mostly by what comes out of the mouth of those people. Hitler was intelligent. *Is he admired and respected by the vast majority of people?* Personally, I don't grant   intelligence with the highest mark in the list of human attributes. Intelligence, of course, is extremely important but it has to work in collaboration with the heart.

Teachers encourage discrimination

The students with less than a B are discriminated against by the teachers, first, and often by the A and B students, after. They are seen as brainless and that belief is encouraged by the school system. They are constantly belittled and humiliated. They are seen as inferior and dumb, in spite of the fact that it's seldom the case. They are most of the time students who are aware that the school system sucks and they are not motivated. A lack of motivation is most of the time interpreted as laziness.

School imposes artificial curiosity.

School compromises kids' innate curiosity, which, in turn, diminishes their appetite for learning and thus their creativity.

Kids get born with an innate curiosity. They have a strong impulse to learn. They also have an endless creativity. We don't need to push them to learn or create. They want to learn. Learning is one of the greatest sources of pleasure in life. So by nature, if we don't tamper with their innate curiosity, they will learn constantly and learn what is propitious to their self-actualization. They will also create games, toys, plays etc. They won't need any exterior motivations or coaxing. Motivation and coaxing will only interfere with their natural propensity to fulfill their own potential and establish their own self.

When we condemn them to go to school, we put their own appetite for learning on standby. Suddenly, we tell them what they have to be curious about and shut down their own curiosity for 6-7 hours a day, 5 days a week. If they don't conform to that unnatural rule, they get punished. Gradually, they start to lessen their innate curiosity to avoid being coerced. They betray who they really are, to satisfy the rules of a system they learn to distrust and dislike. Most will end up hating school and learning

Society thinks that kids need to be redesigned and modified to be ok.

"The essential is to be what nature made us; we're always too much what men want us to be."

(Author's translation from French)

— Jean-Jacques Rousseau

A child is the most complete book of anthropology ever written. We should study the ingenuity and the complexity of a child. All he needs is love and respect. With that, he will grow up to become autonomous and a real humanist, school or no school, preferably not the schools as we know them. André Moreau, a French philosopher from Québec, said *that "kids would know what to do if we didn't first teach them what not to do."* We raise them so they fit in society. They shouldn't. It's not a sign of success to fit a society like ours.

"Man get born naturally good, society corrupts him." (Author's translation from French)

— Jean Jacques Rousseau

CHAPTER 4

Coercion

"If we wish to preserve a free society, it is essential that we recognize that the desirability of a particular object is not sufficient justification for the use of coercion."

— Friedrich August von Hayek

The word "coercion" is a word dotted of so many components that it would fill many books by itself. I'll try to address a few of its most common components. Google gives this definition of coercion: *"the practice of persuading someone to do something by using force or threats."*

In most cases, it starts in the family, from a very young age. The child starts walking around one year old. There are things that he shouldn't touch because of the danger for himself or the risk of breaking something the parents value. The words *"don't touch!"* do not always accomplish the desired result. So the parent increases the tone of the warning or grab the kid and pulls him away or, in some cases, slaps the hand of the child gently to make the kid understand that he cannot touch certain things that are within his reach.

We, as parents tend to excuse the use of an unpleasant deterrent by using the excuse that it is for his safety first and his education, second. He must learn to differentiate his things from *other people's things. His rights, from the rights of others.* But a one-year-old or a two or three-year-old doesn't have the concept of right or wrong. Right is what his parents put up with and wrong what they reprimand him for. He's too young to have a proper understanding of right versus wrong. It will take many more years before he can grasp the sense of that elusive concept. And he will only grasp it, if his parents have themselves a truly realistic concept of justice and morality. Otherwise, their efforts will only lead to confusion.

"The principle that human nature, in its psychological aspects, is nothing more than a product of history and given social relations removes all barriers to coercion and manipulation by the powerful."

— Noam Chomsky

Coercion has become so intertwined in our interaction with others that we, most of the time, are not aware that we're using that powerful weapon. We give it all kinds of noble names, like discipline, control, education, civilization, obedience, attentiveness, tough love, caring, responsibility etc. We use it as an excuse for disrespecting our children and others. We also use it for pushing kids to conformism, to subjugation, to betrayal of self, to submission to blind obedience and to prostitution of self, in order to avoid disapproval of others.

There are a few examples of the excuses we use to justify the exaggerate use of coercion. When we use coercion with our kids, what message are we really giving them? "I'll cease to like you or even to love you if you don't obey my demands, whatever they are. I'll yell at you, ground you, send you to your room, take your cell phone away from you, etc."

After having done those things 20 times without positive results, why do we continue doing it? After we told our teenager to do his homework 4 times and he didn't do it, what makes us think that the fifth or the sixth time will work? Wouldn't it be easier to let our child take the responsibility of his homework and take the consequences at school? How do kids become responsible? Not that I believe that they should do their homework; I don't!

Homework is one of the most stupid practices of our school system. It's totally useless, fruitless, and punitive. It's a form of long distance coercion. After the kid has spent 6 or 7 hours bolted to a seat, listening to mostly useless indoctrination, which, most of the time, isn't age appropriate, where does the teacher take the gull to go outside of the walls of the school to somehow infiltrate his private life? What right do they have to poison the kids free time at home, time they need desperately to recuperate from the mental drudgery of their day at school?

Our school system is archaic, primitive, and destructive of our youth. It is destructive in a myriad of ways. It puts on hold their innate curiosity. It bombards their mind with instructions about which they're not interested in the least bit. It uses threats and blackmailing constantly in order to save them in spite of themselves, it seems.

We're in the 21st century. In America, a percentage of the population, knows that the school system is limping tragically. But in order to improve the school system, it would cost money and the government doesn't want to spent more money. The government doesn't care about the school system's humanistic value. They compare it to that of the other countries and brainwash us into believing that we're doing better than the average, which means nothing, in reality. We're doing better academically, period. That, to me, means nothing. Academics are related to instruction; not education.

What we should want for our kids are schools on the model of the Quality Schools created and implemented by William Glasser around 25-30 years ago in the United States and eventually in some other countries, but on a small scale. In his book, *The Quality Schools, managing students without coercion*, he explains clearly how to convert regular schools into Quality Schools.

Managing students without coercion is for me the largest achievement of humanity in the last thousand years. Sorry, but man walking on the moon never impressed me. Quite on the contrary, we haven't learned how to put one foot in front of the other on the earth and *we dare brag about having set foot on the moon?* Shame on us!

Chapter 5

The mind

"More compassionate mind, more sense of concern for other's well-being, is source of happiness."

— Dalai Lama

What exactly is the so called mind? Is it like the hard drive on our PC? I believe it's more complex than the hard drive. This last one only memorizes bits of information. The mind remembers things, but reflects about them, the way they are and the way we would like them to be. Our mind is selective and reasons about the value of the info we have and about the way we should use that info for our benefit and that of others. Our mind ponders possibilities and events. It makes choices among the options better suited to our ideals. *The mind has a mind of its own...*

Now, depending on the way our parents will relate to us, we will end up with a few possible attitudes and quirks of our mind. If our parents are conformists and religious, we will grow up to become like them in most of the cases, in most departments of life. We will accept their religion and copy their brown nosing the establishment. We will become dumbed down by the influence of the school system and become *"good"* citizens. We will fit in society and make our parents proud of themselves for having succeeded so well in their parents' duties.

If our parents are nonconformists and non religious, we will grow up to become like them in most of the cases, in most departments of life. We will decide if we want to join a certain religion –or not- without our parents interfering in our decision. Chance is we'll not find a religion that suits our sense of self-actualization and freedom. We will not like school, but probably choose to take the best we can out of it –or not- and our parents will not be on our case about our homework or our performing at school. They will support us in our choices.

On the other hand, they will not run around to catch the rocks we're throwing in the air above our heads. Rather they will trust that we'll learn from our experiences. They'll do that, because the only true knowledge is the one we acquire with experiences. That kind of knowledge takes a long time to acquire and is very painful at times, but it's priceless, compared to academia's pseudo-knowledge.

More and more with the advent of cybernetics, everybody of the young generation carries all the knowledge of the world in a little enchanted box they call a smart phone. It's like a magic wand; they just have to type any question they might have, and they get the answer faster than any human teacher could deliver. Why in the world would they bother listening to boring information, hours on end, and try to memorize it?

One day, somebody asked Einstein the formula of the law of gravity. To that person's surprise, he answered he didn't know it.

''How can you not know it, retorted the interlocutor, *you discovered that law and made it known to the world?''*

To what Einstein replied: *"Never memorize something that you can look up."*

In other words, why would he bother remembering

something he can find in the dictionary and encumber his brain for nothing?

Of course, he remembered that formula, but he wanted to remind us of the importance of the mind for creating instead of simply storing bits of information. The mind is curious, playful, ingenious, creative, and nearly unlimited. Imagination is a very powerful tool that is at the root of most inventions.

"Imagination is not only the uniquely human capacity to envision that which is not, and, therefore, the foundation of all invention and innovation. In its arguably most transformative and revelatory capacity, it is the power that enables us to empathize with humans whose experiences we have never shared."

— J.K. Rowling

CHAPTER 6

The Gate of the Mind

"It is the mark of an educated mind to be able to entertain a thought without accepting it."

— Aristotle

To put it bluntly, to humanize ourselves, we must design and install a ***"built-in bullshit detector"*** at the gates of our mind, as soon as possible in life. We shouldn't believe anything we hear. We should only accept what we heard as a belief, after thorough examination and the conviction that the content is favorable to our journey, to our pursuit of humanization; humanization of self and of others.

"It is not enough to have a good mind; the main thing is to use it well."

— René Descartes

The mind is gullible, hungry and greedy. It catches whatever comes its way if you don't have in place that precious *B.S. detector*. The mind is expendable. It can never be filled. But the fuller it is, the more it can become confused by the clutter of useless information and pseudo-knowledge. If I remember that Christopher Columbus discovered America in 1492 – which, by the way, is not true, - and I don't remember my wife's birthday, there's going to be hardships to deal with…

I predict that in a not so distant future, school will stop teaching academic subjects to students. With the smart phones in everybody's hands, information in class has become obsolete and a total waste of time and patience on the part of students. There is no teacher that can compete with computer's information in speed and in accuracy of the content. I believe that it's very possible that the tree of the knowledge of good and evil, the tree in the Garden of Eden, they talked about in the bible, was a computer that aliens showed to primitive people of that era. These primitive people didn't have words to describe it better than the tree of knowledge. Maybe it was an Apple (computer) tree...

"Look and think before opening the shutter. The heart and mind are the true lens of the camera."

— Yousuf Karsh

Your mind configuration is yours to plan, to design and to precisely construct in a way that you will naturally choose to act with love for yourself and for others. There lies the secret of humanization. Our nature wants that and knows how to get there, *if we remove the garbage that was dumped in our minds in the first part of our life and that we have to remove in order to be functional and fully humane.*

It's tempting for parents to indoctrinate their children with all their beliefs and customs; in other words, with their culture, good and bad. People don't usually see anything wrong with the culture transmitted to them by their parents. The parents who practice arranged marriages, don't realize that such a custom is as disrespectful as it is stupid and cruel. That represents an ownership total of their children, in their beliefs and in their way of raising their children that borders on barbarism.

Where did such a custom come from? Probably it was

related to the economic standing of families trying to use marriage to their capitalist interest and using the children to achieve their goal. As long as it was a matter of survival, it can be understood. The problem is that, due to the socio-cultural inertia or the fear of change, that primitive practice is still used in modern days, while the survival motivation doesn't exist anymore. It's a sign of being stuck in the past and not wanting to accept the unavoidable changes of our modern society.

That is an example of what the gate of the mind should block, examine its social and moral value and make the appropriate choice of dumping the obsolete custom. There again, with the majority of people, we don't find yet the installation of such a screening device at the entrance of the mind. We will possibly find it in greater frequency among the young generation who is in the process of disconnecting with the past and live in the present/future new world order. (No connection with the club of the same name…)

Chapter 7

Education

"Our progress as a nation can be no swifter than our progress in education. The human mind is our fundamental resource."

— John F. Kennedy

The word "education" is on every lip, but has a different meaning for different people. Most of the time when people talk about education, they mean instruction or a certain acquisition of information. For me, it means an attempt at helping people to acquire a certain development of certain faculties allowing them to self-actualize and become their true self. It's not to add content, it's to help strengthen the mind, sharpen the mind, humanize the mind and therefore themselves. Any accomplishment from the person originates in the mind and is the result of a choice in the course of actions.

We should not confuse intelligence and mindfulness. Intelligence is a tool, a magnificent tool at that. But intelligence by itself has no discernment, no moral. It allows us to accomplish a lot of tasks, but not necessarily tasks that are beneficial to us and others. A chainsaw is a great and powerful tool. You can cut all kinds of trees on your property with it and on anybody else's property. It's not selective. It will cut whatever you aim it at. Your mind is there to remind you that you cannot cut any tree that is on other people's property, or even cut a tree that is on your property but will land in the neighbor's backyard. Being very intelligent doesn't come automatically with common sense. For that, you need to work on your mind, to expurgate it of any indoctrination and to install the **built-in bullshit detector** mentioned before.

"Skepticism: the mark and even the pose of the educated mind."

— John Dewey

When I Google "mind" and "intelligence", I disagree with its definition of intelligence. I do not believe that intelligence by itself, without education, provides judgment and discernment. It defines both as having: *understanding, reasoning, judgment, sense, head.* The mind can be greatly improved, educated, sharpened, etc. The level of intelligence or someone's I.Q. doesn't increase much during his lifetime, however hard one tries to increase it. The mind, on the other hand, is nearly limitless in its ability to be modified, improved, orientated and life changing.

Love of self and of others, of life, of nature, understanding, comprehension, empathy, passion for arts etc. comes from the mind, or from the heart, as we often say; not from the intelligence. Intelligence has no feelings. The mind coached by the heart is the powerful source of everything good we witness around us. All creativity uses intelligence and the mind. But the fruits of creativity are not all beneficial. The holocaust was very creative in its conception, but very destructive in its execution

"To be creative means to connect. It's to abolish the gap between the body, the mind and the soul, between science and art, between fiction and nonfiction."

— Nawal El Saadawi

What is positive education?

The ultimate education is the one you receive or should receive at home. I say "should" because the art of educating children is the most important and consequential of all arts. At the same time, it's an art that has been largely adulterated and compromised during the course of history. In America, -and in most countries- the culture, including religion, has tempered with the maternal instinct to the point that the natural instinct has been straight jacketed to fit the ambient culture. Women have not lost their instinct; they have gradually, under the pressure of their culture, resigned themselves to adopt a misguided way of raising their children to satisfy the social pressure. This new accommodating maternal instinct is not fulfilling all the emotional needs of the infant and of the growing child later.

One of the most damaging culture interference in the mother child relationship is the partial abandon of the **absolute essential need of breastfeeding the infant.** This vital function is not negotiable in nature and should not be negotiable in our society. We have to find a way to allow and encourage women to breastfeed their infant for at least one year. They should receive full salary for that year, given the respect women deserve when they accomplish such an important function, both for the infant and for themselves.

Society forces them to hide when they breastfeed like if it was somehow related to sex. There's nothing sexual about breastfeeding. And 1 believe that men's misogynistic attitude is the cause for such an incomprehensible behavior. I strongly believe that religions have played a large role in that regrettable and unnatural new behavior of too many mothers.

First, one has to be prude to see in breastfeeding something that must be hidden from people's view. It has no more reason to be hidden from the view of people than the action of a person eating food at the table. They are both feeding themselves to curb their hunger in order to survive.

I have been asking myself if the Catholic Church played a role in that unnatural pursuit due to their obsession for women's modesty. Or could it be that somehow they found out that nursing mothers had less chance of getting pregnant the longer they breastfed their infant? Women can go over a year, without ovulating if they also breastfeed during the night. And, when the infant reaches six months of age, they can introduce solid food as a supplement and continue breastfeeding.

"La revenge des berceaux" which translates by the revenge of the cradles was an expression in catholic Quebec meaning that, by encouraging women to have as many kids as they could, there would be more French Canadians than English peoples in Quebec. This way, they thought there would be more Catholics than Protestants, *ipso facto*. Women in catholic countries are not allowed to use birth control of any kind except abstinence, even to this day! Is it possible that the Catholic Church made breastfeeding awkward in order to have women abandon the practice after a few months and get pregnant sooner instead of continuing to breastfeed and thus possibly delaying pregnancy for over a year?

I don't think that a woman can do anything more

important for the infant's physical and mental health than breastfeeding him for as long as possible. There's no gadget or new scientific discovery that will ever replace or surpass the value of breastfeeding for both the infant and the mother.

I believe that mothers that have not been adulterated by ambient culture have much better chance to raise their kids properly. If you allow me to use an example, I will speculate that if my mother had caught me or one of my brothers masturbating, it would have been a real drama. She was programmed by the catholic religion to threaten us with hell and make us feel terrible. A normal un-indoctrinated mother should walk away with a smile on her face and give the child privacy.

Masturbation is normal, 100% natural and perfectly acceptable for anybody that feels the need or enjoys the pleasure of sexual release. One *doesn't get blind, grow hair in the palm of his hands* or other manipulative fallacies of the kind. I would guess that 95% of the people who have been raised catholic do masturbate but still feel a certain amount of guilt. And that, even if they have abandoned the catholic religion a long time ago. It shows that indoctrination, reinforced with coercion, leaves long term scars on the psyche and some of them more serious than the guilt about sexual gratification.

The worse scars are probably coming from the deception of having been lied to, in order to achieve compliance, by our parents at home, by the teachers in school, by the priests in church and by the authorities in society at large. Traumas are traumas. Traumas of that magnitude, on children, leave a real deep scar on their mind and soul.

Let's suppose you go in your yard and bend a small tree with an inch diameter trunk, and secure it in that bent position for a few years. Then you find out that it was not a nice thing to do to the tree. Your excuses to the tree and the removal of the bending gismo will not erase the stress caused by your action and the tree will not swing back in its original straight up position instantly, or ever!

An arborist looking at that tree could explain to you that the tree will always show signs of the original stress imposed on its trunk and, by consequence, on the branches that need a proper circulation of the sap towards their aerial roots. The branches need that *"breastfeeding"* of sort that comes from the roots and get dispensed to the branches so that they will produce leaves which, in turn,   produce oxygen for you and me to breathe.

So in the example of the bent tree, the more severe is the bend, the more serious the negative effects will be for the branches or *the tree's children*. The same applies to our children. The parents' coercive ways of educating their children will leave scars on their children proportionate to *the sharpness of the bend forced on their young pliable psyche.* There are no religions, no school systems, no political systems, in a word, no kind of education worth sacrificing the true nature of a child and his virgin brain and soul!

With its horrible and destructive teachings, the catholic church pressured my mother into alienating and scaring us. All that in the name of an infinitely loving God! I hope one day the catholic religion will be recognized as one of the most damaging religion ever invented and imposed on ignorant primitive people to control them and take advantage of them, in the cruelest fashion possible. That religion is possibly the strongest motivation for atheism there is. Some might tell me that my mother didn't have to submit to the church's fairy tales... That's how my next chapter's title got born.

CHAPTER 8

Culture: the hidden trap.

"Change will come slowly, across generations, because old beliefs die hard even when demonstrably false."

— E. O. Wilson

While everybody praises and values their culture, I happen to have a very different opinion of that concept. For me, culture has left a bad taste in my soul. Some might retort to me that it was not the culture *per se* that poisoned my youth, but that it was the way my parents chose to impose certain parts of it on me. They did it with the best of intentions, not realizing that what they were imposing on me was against nature and was poisoning my life.

Eventually, I got out from under the dictatorial yoke that was crushing me -and them- relentlessly. *Culture "is transmitted, through language, material objects, ritual, institutions and art, from one generation to the next."*

www.dictionary.com/browse/culture

That definition of culture found on the web is very much what I think of the way culture survives the change of time through centuries.

I would however like to add a comment I feel important for you the reader. When it says rightly that it is transmitted through institutions, I would like to list what institutions are most apt to transmit the culture than others. First, I put the family, Second, the religion. Third, the school. Fourth, the people. Fifth, the government and, in the last 50 years, the media, carriers of propaganda and consumerism ideology, among other things.

I will not deny that the culture played a role in the evolution of humanity. I can't say for sure if it was a motivational role or a deterrent towards humanization. In the 21st century, the rules of the game have been forever changed. We should not consider our culture as a value to hold onto in its entirety and to transmit as is to the coming generation. Looking back and hanging onto what has brought us up to the present day, can only prolong the *disarray* where humanity is finding itself at the moment. Clinging to certain parts of the culture is like driving a car at 100 kms per hour while looking mainly in the rear view mirror. The chances of arriving at destination without accidents are from infinitely slim to non-existent.

Clinging to our culture is a major and misguided way of avoiding taking the risk of maybe going a step further towards the humanization of man. It's a mistake humankind has repeated for millenniums, which cop-out it refuses to see and to admit. It's choosing a highway to destruction or at least the turtle pace towards advancement of man. It's the coward way of facing the challenge that besieges every man on the road to self-actualization.

In a lecture on culture and human progress, Radha Burnier said that *"civilizations decline because of the infatuation of people with their past. Satisfied with their previous achievements, they display apathy and incompetence in coping with the challenge of the present. It is obviously important to keep the mind and heart free from past burdens and memories of achievement; specializations which may have been assets in the past no longer remain helpful for further progress.*

If we keep telling people what they like to hear, chance is that we repeat to them what they already know. It's not challenging and it doesn't threaten their peace of mind. They prefer to remain in the overused trail borrowed by the majority, than the new path that is offered to them. They could create for themselves and others who have the courage to try something new a path with unknown curves and pitfalls which is possibly promising a better outcome than the old sterile and hopeless trail.

**("*The sum of attitudes, customs, and beliefs that distinguishes one group of people from another.)*

"Freedom of the mind is essential for the flowering of culture. A free mind looks not merely through one narrow window, but has an all-round vision with no frontiers. A civilization which imprisons itself within the known frontiers of knowledge and experience stagnates and brings about its own decline."

— *Radha Burnier*

To tell a people that culture is not all it's thought to be, is a daring undertaking. It's their security blanket. It's for them a tool of identification and of valorization. It differentiates them from "the others" and, in their mind, puts them a few notches above any other people. In this way it becomes a tool of segregation instead of a tool of unification and cohesion to the humanity as a whole

I'm aware that I'm a nonconformist to the hilt. First, I look at the family, our sacred institution, with no reproaches, but with worries. Most of our families use coercion to control their kids. Coercion is never beneficial:

at home, in school, in church, at work, in the community or anywhere else for that matter. Coercion is damaging people's self-image and promotes resentment and often hatred from its victims towards the perpetrators.

I consider our school system as archaic and as a deterrent to our kids' self-actualization. In that way, it's destructive towards our kids. I maintain that the catholic religion is tyrannical, preaches fairy tales, and presents an image of God that should turn everybody into atheists or, at least, agnostics. Its God is mean, vengeful and built on the image of man with his weaknesses.

What I'll tell you next will not please everybody. I also consider all religions as a deterrent to humanization. They are divisive. They encourage an "us" versus the "others" kind of mentality. They also encourage people to maintain the *status quo*, which, most of the time, promotes socio-cultural inertia.

CHAPTER 9

Religion

"Religion is regarded by the common people as true, by the wise as false, and by the rulers as useful."

— Lucius Annaeus Seneca

Trying to separate religion from culture is futile. We inherit the religion of our fathers as an inherent part of our culture. Of all the components of a transmitted culture, religion has a particular slant to it. Although culture is by nature a controlling force, religion is by far the most powerful tool of population control ever concocted.

Once people have been properly indoctrinated, you don't have to watch them in order to make sure they follow the beaten trail. The coercive teaching and brainwashing they have been victims of is like a whip always following them and forcing them to behave the way the authority has indoctrinated them to do. After all, *"God is watching them and will throw them in hell for eternity"* if they transgress the law. The more people are fearful of God, the more the authority can control and subjugate them to their own rules.

"Religion, comprises a system of wishful illusions together with a disavowal of reality, such as we find in an isolated form nowhere else but in amentia, in a state of blissful hallucinatory confusion."

— Sigmund Freud

I despise religion for many reasons. First for what it did to my mother who let them tell her what to do with her mind, her body and the mind and the body of her children.

My mother wanted TWO kids, as she told me when she was 78 years old. I'm the fifteenth kid in the family… **What's up with that?** She had to hide from everybody, even from the other young kids, to breastfeed her babies. Somehow it was something related to sex …or sinful. She had to hide in her bedroom to make sure other children of whatever age wouldn't see such an intimate …or maybe a sexual and devious action!

Some will tell me it was culture and not religion that pushed her to such a weird behavior. It's possible but how do you separate the two, and which one is predominant in the mix? There's also the possibility that the misogynistic attitude of man has forced women into such a bizarre behavior. Why would men care about women's breasts being seen by other people? Would it be instead that they do not want other men to see their woman's breasts, by jealousy and the need to control their woman to keep them under their thumb at all time?

In any event, the result is the same. We're in the 21st century and breastfeeding is still considered like something you do in the privacy of your bedroom. And we have been to the moon, they say! For me, there is only one stupid animal in the creation and it's man! It sounds disrespectful and dumb to advance something as untrue as that. Of course when I say that man is the only stupid animal in the creation, I don't mean it *verbatim*. Here's what I mean. Man is capable of achieving a much more advanced civilization than he has. A more advanced civilization implying increased humanization, which would be beneficial to everybody. Man knows how to do it. My question is why didn't he do it in the last ten thousand years? My answer is simple.

Man has been manipulated since the beginning of times by power hungry leaders. Man is scared of the unknown. Man is gullible. Man is easily seduced by promises of future happiness. The promise of heaven is the best example I can choose. Man is easily scared by the threat of catastrophes, the devil, mad gods …or hell.

Most of us now know that there's no such things as devils, mad gods and hell. Why is it that we're still subjugated to the status quo and so slow in the advancement of humanization?

Could man have lost hope of ever instituting a real democracy and not a government of elected dictators as we now have? Could man have started to believe that real civilization and peace are an utopia? Has man given up on the humanization of people, relying instead on God to interfere and somehow put it in place for them?

"The same people that wrote the bible   thought the world was flat."

~ Unknown – (disputed)

I don't know for sure if there is a God, but one thing I do know. If there's a God, He will not interfere in the world affairs to solve for us problems we have created and don't have the courage to solve. If God exists and He created humanity, He knew what He was doing and doesn't have to come and fix whatever we broke. We cannot surprise Him with our weaknesses and our clumsiness. He designed us the way we are and, in that way, we are perfectly designed in accordance with His plan.

The strongest tool of the Christian churches is their teaching of the creation of hell by God. That, to me, is the backbone of Christian religions. It's probably the smartest part of their fairy tale… It has given them a level of power over people never seen before and never to be seen again. It's the equivalent of a magic wand, a super demonic whip of gargantuan proportion: *the threat of hell!* It's a bit like being put in isolation in a jail but a lot more sophisticated and vicious. The isolation hole is a huge furnace filled with other miserable humans like you! And the clock is set on: *forever*. God is full of surprises, isn't He

"I cannot imagine a God who rewards and punishes the objects of his creation, whose purposes are modeled after our own -- a God, in short, who is but a reflection of human frailty. Neither can I believe that the individual survives the death of his body, although feeble souls harbor such thoughts through fear or ridiculous egotism."

— Einstein

CHAPTER 10

Humanization

"I think there is a tendency for people to get rigid and caught up in their beliefs of what is right and wrong, and they lose sight of humanity. Being human has to come first before right or wrong."

⊠ Matisyahu

People have been going to church on Sunday for centuries. They have prayed to God and the saints also for centuries. Is society any better than it was 1000 years ago? Do people apply the *"do unto others as they would like them do unto them"* more than they were a 1000 years ago? Are there less wars and aggressions between countries than there was then?

I don't think religions work now more than they ever did. So, why are all those demonstrations of piety for? Could it be purely and simply bold hypocrisy? With the rapid advance of computer technology, there is a new god around and it is called "cybernetics". The cell phone more and more dominates the preoccupation of more than half the world population with communications. It's more than a religion; it's an obsession! It's not mainly or solely on Sunday morning; it's all day and part of the night, seven days a week. Should we be concerned about its effect on this generation and the coming ones?

The era of communications is in its infancy. Started with the advent of the telegraph for certain companies, followed with the "talking telegraph" or telephone in 1849, it has made the industrial revolution a lot easier and faster. In the next 150 years, the phone became part of the everyday's preferred instrument of communication. From the house phone bolted to the wall to the pocket phone, the *revolutionary cell phone* appeared and brought the future in the now!

It's a new fad, a new gadget. It's evolving very fast and will be replaced by even more incredible and exciting gadgets. For the old generation, it's kind of a shock to see everybody on their cell when they meet for a lunch at the fast food restaurant or even while driving or in class or at work sometime.

That we like it or not, it's here to stay. It's trying to warn us that yesterday is gone and that we have just entered a new era, a new world. The world as we knew it is no more. All our sacred institutions are subject to a major transformation. The traditional family composed of a man and a woman with 5 to 15 kids is now replaced with a man and a woman most of the time, or two men or two women, some of the time, with one to three kids. Fifty four percent of marriages fall apart with the kids having to commute from Mom's to Dad's place.

The religions are falling apart in many major countries of which Canada is an example. In the province of Québec, the attendance to the Catholic Church has passed from over 90%, 30-40 years ago, to under 10% now. Churches are closing down and are getting sold and, sometimes, converted into condominiums etc. In B.C., it's now around 30% practicing. It's the end of an era. We're facing a new world order of sort.

School as we knew it is gradually changing. In less than 10 years, I believe that there will be no more teachers in most classes at the secondary level, except for extracurricular activities like theatre, music, sculpture etc. Teaching the academic subjects of the curriculum is useless and a waste of time. Information doesn't come from the teacher anymore but from the internet.

Why fill kids' heads with any information they're not interested in, when they can find it in 10 seconds if and when they want it or need it? So the family is falling apart, the religions are seriously dwindling. The school system we have known is on the point of dramatically being transformed. The next big institution remaining is the government.

With people abandoning the traditional religions and the decline of the brainwashing and subjugation it was imposing on the population, I believe that more and more people will demand a more genuine democracy to replace the "elected dictatorship" which, until now , we have put up with.

Everywhere we turn to, we see a rapid revolution of all our institutions and social systems. The dehumanizing influence of the religions being more and more a thing of the past, we might see, for the first time in our lifetime, a movement of people aiming tentatively towards an increased humanization of the world.

For humanism also appeals to man as man. It seeks to liberate the universal qualities of human nature from the narrow limitations of blood and soil and class and to create a common language and a common culture in which men can realize their common humanity.

— Christopher Dawson

CHAPTER 11

Public schools

"I think schools generally do an effective and terribly damaging job of teaching children to be infantile, dependent, intellectually dishonest, passive and disrespectful to their own developmental capacities."

— Seymour Papert

Tempering with the students' beliefs.

"The teacher knows everything. He is smarter than them. He has the power to transmit knowledge to them. He is a good person. He never lies. He is honest. The students can't make it in life without his limitless knowledge. He holds the key to their future success and happiness. He wants what's best for them. He always respects them even when he is brainwashing them. He cares about them. He knows everything about kids etc." That is the general consensus of indoctrinated people. We use propaganda to make students believe that it is so. In reality, everybody knows that most of it is like election promises...

What the teacher believes he is teaching:

Maths, chemistry, biology, history, geography, social sciences, languages, phys ed etc.

What the teacher is really teaching students:

To obey without questioning the validity of the orders. To hate learning: learning what they don't have curiosity for or interest in. To lie to themselves: *"if I quit school, my parents will kill me. If I get a grade 12 diploma, I'll be successful and happy."* To become masochistic: to put up with abuse they could and should reject. To compensate for their boredom with destructive habits: smoking, street drugs, overeating, overuse of gadgets, risky sex practices etc.

Forcing their attention via coercion.

Our public school system is made possible with two factors. One, it's decreed by the government as a law. Two, by law, kids between the age of 6 and 16 are legally obliged to attend school. Their bodies must be in class for 6 periods a day, 5 days a week. That much the school can achieve 99% of the time.

As for their minds, that's a different ball game. The attendance of the mind is only partial and part of the time. Only the "A" students bring their minds in the classroom with them most of the time and at maybe a percentage of participation of over 90% of the time. Those numbers are not scientifically proven. The teacher cannot transmit knowledge if the minds are not there and *motivated* to learn. He must therefore find a way to accomplish that feat.

"*Our school system does not educate; it indoctrinates.*" Indoctrination is best achieved through repetitions of certain teachings, mantras or doctrines. The best tool to make it possible is coercion. In the church, we use the threat of hell as a whip to keep people in line and have them accept the imposed doctrines. In school, we use the threats of expulsion, flunking, visits to the principal, suspensions or even corporal punishments in some countries. In other words, it's brainwashing achieved through blackmailing.

"Most teachers waste their time by asking questions which are intended to discover what a pupil does not know, whereas the true art of questioning has for its purpose to discover what the pupil knows or is capable of knowing." "...I never teach my pupils. I only attempt to provide the conditions in which they can learn."

— Eisntein

CHAPTER 12

Beliefs: a double edge dagger.

"The task of the modern era was the realization and humanization of God – the transformation and dissolution of theology into anthropology."
— Ludwig Feuerbach

Around 15 years ago, I came across an article on the web that got my attention about beliefs and their very versatile influence on us.

Here's a story about what happened to a young medical student who was hitchhiking to get to his destination as cheaply as possible. He decided to bum a ride on a freight train. So he jumps in a wagon going in the right direction with his pack sack. He closes the door of the wagon and lights up a candle to write in his diary. That's when he notices, spelled out on the end wall: REFRIGERATED WAGON!!! He gets up, picks up his pack sack, goes to open the door to jump off the wagon; the door has locked itself from the outside. *Oh God! He's trapped in this walk-in refrigerator! He panics. What will happen to him?*

He begins to calculate how many hours he has to spend in that critical situation before the train arrives at its destination and he gets to be freed. Can he survive the duration of this grim journey?

He worries with good reasons; he feels increasingly cold. He writes in his diary how he feels as the hours pass. Stiffness is invading his limbs; death is whirling above his head like a buzzard. He's going to fall asleep, he knows, *never to wake up*!

He was found dead the next day or the day after, with the record of the progression of his death, victim of the cold. *He had indeed died from the cold.* However, I must add that there was no food in the wagon needing to be kept cold. Consequently, *the refrigerating system was not activated.*

His belief, his conviction that he would die frozen had killed him, not the temperature in the wagon, which was well above the freezing point.

"Believe or not to believe, that's the question!"

That anecdote explains the choice of this paragraph's title. In our conversations, the words "I believe that…" comes more often than most other affirmations like "I know that…", "I feel that…", "I don't know…" etc. We affirm that we believe a lot of things. Do we really believe these things or did they get grafted in our mind by other people like parents and teachers when we were young and we automatically repeat these things like robots without really consciously believing them?

When in chapter 6, I said that we must design and install a *"built-in bullshit detector"* at the gates of the mind, as soon as possible in life, I was not joking. I couldn't be more serious. I repeat myself here, but I insist, we shouldn't believe anything we hear. We should only accept what we heard as a belief after thorough examination and conviction that the content is favorable to our journey, to our pursuit of humanization; humanization of self and of others.

Beliefs are the number one force that runs the world. Nothing else is even close to the influence that our beliefs have on our life. Knowledge doesn't even get close to compete with beliefs in the pursuit of our life. Knowledge is comprised of a bank of information units which most of the time are unproven or partially false. That everybody believe something has no bearing on its truthfulness!

That we all believe that Christopher Columbus discovered America doesn't change the fact that it's completely false or that we don't have a clue who really did discover America! It's only something that was written in our history books and imposed on us when we were too young to question the validity of that information. It's the same with most of what we hold as the truth because a book said so. Most of history is seasoned with falsehood, most of the time injected by purpose by a country to gain prestige in front of the world.

If you have the time and want an example of what I'm talking about, check the web for an article called: *6 Ridiculous Lies You Believe About the Founding of America*. I don't have any proof that what it claims is true, but it tickles my neurons in a soothing way…

If I had my say in the public school system's choice of a curriculum, I would really hesitate in having history as part of it. And if I would keep it in the curriculum, I would warn the students that most of what they are going to read is in large part dubious and sometimes false.

If we try to learn how to eat right by listening to TV programs on proper diet, we're losing our time. First, they change their recommendations about the best food every 8 to 10 years. For years we've been told that whole wheat bread was the staff of life. That milk was great for everybody. I could go on, but let's look at these two food items. Wheat is not recommended anymore. You surely heard about the book *Wheat Bellies*. As for milk, lots of people are allergic to it and *there's milk and milk...*

Unless you buy complete milk, you're drinking processed milk that might be poison in some countries. In order to make more money with a certain amount of milk, some companies buy milk from which the cream and anything else that was edible have been removed. They add water to increase the volume of that milk, to a point that it's like bluish water. And to bring it back to its original color and density, they add a variety of chemicals including substance like *urea, detergent, refined oil, caustic soda and white paint!* That is what has been found in 88% of a certain country's milk. And before we throw the rock at them, it's not unique to their country.

Granted that cow urine is considered a powerful drug against a variety of health problems including cancer, by certain people, we're definitely not familiar with the practice. That they extract the urea from that urine and add it to water down milk might be beneficial even if in America we might think that it's a primitive people's superstition. But I won't reject that practice as stupid because to us it seems stupid. You can see for yourself if you Google: *Cow Urine Promoted for Health Benefits.*

It could very well be 100% true and beneficial. Most of us don't think so, but most of us don't know so. That all the people in the world believe that something is true or wrong doesn't add or remove any truthfulness from that something. Facts are facts whatever we think about them.

However, when I read that they add *caustic soda and white paint* to that mixture, it raises a warning sign in my brain. So I checked on the web to get a second opinion in the matter. To my question: Is caustic soda edible? I got this answer:

"No it is not - caustic soda is very alkaline and even a small amount ingested will burn your digestive system and kill."

Yahoo Answers

As for the white paint, I don't have to check. I'm very familiar with paint, white or other, and it's not edible. We could mix some ingredients together and maybe end up with a product that when applied on a surface would turn that surface a different color when dry. It would look like we painted that surface. But would it resist the wear and tear or the weather as well as paint does? I doubt it, but I cannot say that it wouldn't just because I don't believe it could.

Now I have a dilemma. India is a very progressive country and very advanced in computer technology. Is it a sign of ignorance on their part or is it a trick that allows the milk industry to make more money? I believe that it's a trick to make more money.

I certainly have a problem with adulteration of food to increase profits. That kind of practice is used largely in the world, and maybe in an excessive way in the United States and in China.

In America *"the pure"*, we must be aware of the genetically modified organisms, or GMOs, which increases the yield of the crops. There would be as *many* as 30,000 different GMO products on *grocery* store *shelves in the States...* Are we being genetically modified and gradually becoming "Frankensteinians"? Of course they spend hundreds of millions a year in propaganda denying any ill effects of the GMOs. If we believe them, are we more threatened by the GMO effects or by the uncertainty brought about by their propaganda?

We are possibly not hurt by the GMOs and we're possibly seriously endangered by it. We could be on a one way road where there's no turning back. Man as we know him, the human being as we believe him to have been for millions of years might be on a crashing course with its assumed nature and anthropological make-up.

The chance that we have not yet consumed GMO food items in Canada is nil. There's no law forcing the food magnates in the States to identify GMO products on the label. Lots of our processed food comes from the States. In lots of the processed food they use filler components. You can buy blueberry muffins that contain zero blueberries and at the same time you see in them lots of blueberries that taste like blueberries, look like blueberries but are completely fake.

In order to cut the cost of certain food items like the blueberries in the example above, they use different fillers like corn, soya, and many other fillers that are cheaper, available year round and easier to preserve than fruits, for example.

Among those filler foods, corn and soya are probably the most versatile and the most used GMO fillers. If they can make you eat a zero blueberry muffin and make you believe that it was full of delicious blueberries, they can make you believe that chicken bits are made of 100% chicken. In some cases those delicious bits have zero chicken and 100% filler matter and flavoring in them.

Now, that tempering of food, by substitute matter, might be inoffensive and possibly better than the original food you firmly believe you're eating. We don't know yet. Personally, I like to know what I eat and I research things like GMOs as much as I can on the web. The problem is that we don't necessary find the truth about it. The big corporations using that questionable practice have pretty tight lips about it and about what processed food has been genetically modified. So, for now, we're in the dark.

If you don't know about the substitution and enjoy that food, you're probably better off than if you mistrust and question every bit of food you put in your mouth. The stress caused by your worrying and the fear of damage to your health could possibly cause more problems than the risk incurred by the substitutive products. Again that's an example of how your beliefs can harm you. It's also pure speculation on my part.

Because of the overpopulation of the earth, it's possible that without that practice, which increases the amount of food produced, we could be facing hunger in some countries and more expensive food for everybody because of scarcity. But there again, it's only speculation on my part.

I have given a few examples of beliefs that can- and do- hurt us. Is it to say that we should mistrust our beliefs, become neurotic about it? We must accept that our beliefs are often wrong or damageable to us. But there's one thing that we can believe: we cannot function without beliefs no more than we can garden without having weeds. It's par for the course.

Diamonds come from the earth in a kind of rock we call gangue mineral. It looks like nothing, like junk. If you know how to recognize the type of gangue containing diamonds, you'll take the time and invest in the process of extracting the diamond from it. Not every diamond is precious and valuable, but a lot are. It's the same thing for our beliefs. We must take the time to remove the gangue that covers them all and invest in the process of extracting the precious beliefs and discard the false or worthless ones. Our physical and our emotional welfare depend *"on that bullshit detector accuracy."*

When I say do not believe anything you'll read in this book, it looks like a gimmick or reverse psychology. It's neither. It's me being aware of the risks you take if you believe what I say, without screening it at the entrance of your brain. One is better believe less and miss on some good beliefs than believe too much and be negatively affected by some erratic beliefs.

There would be a lot more to write on such a subject as beliefs, but I think you're getting my point. I don't know that for a fact, but I like to believe you might. And I'm satisfied with that possibility.

CHAPTER 13

Socio-cultural inertia

"The chains of habit are too weak to be felt until they're too strong to be broken."

— Samuel Johnson (1709-1784)

It's generally accepted that we're social animals. Somebody justly said that man is no island. We tend to live in groups that we call tribes, communities or people. What does inertia have to do with societies? If you remember well your physics classes, inertia is the property of masses in motion or at rest to remain in their present state.

Wikipedia define it in this way: **inertia "is the resistance of any physical object to any change in its state of motion (this includes changes to its speed, direction or state of rest). It is the tendency of objects to keep moving in a straight line at constant velocity."**

It's easy to see the analogy between an object resisting a change in its direction and society resisting a change in its beaten trail or its incrusted culture. As members of that society, we're creatures of habit. For some reasons we fear change. Not only do we find it difficult to change some of our habits when we want to, but most of the time, we don't want to. If we believe that premise to be true, why would we oppose change especially when we recognize that it would be beneficial to us?

There's probably more than one cause for that strange

behavior. But in definitive, it's the fear of the unknown versus the comfort of the *status quo* providing us with a kind of security blanket. It's easier to follow the wide and familiar beaten trail than the narrow unfamiliar path of the non-conformist.

We tend to feel more secure following the gang, even when the gang's behavior is destructive, like in the case of oppression, racism and war. **"There's strength in numbers"** is a slogan that is imprinted in our psyche, probably from eons ago. It was probably truer then, than it is now. I tend to believe that it's not the number anymore that provides us real strength, compared to perceived strength.

I rather choose to believe that it's a deprogramming of self and a certain knowledge that can procure us security. Knowledge of self, first and of the other by extension: they're interconnected and interdependent. We can't have one without the other. For me, that's the highest form of knowledge accessible to man. We have been raised hearing a phrase that our religion was pounding us with:

"What good is it for man to conquer the universe if he ends up losing his soul?

I can agree that it isn't worth losing our soul over material gain. However I don't think I have the same definition of soul as they have... Mine comes with a tether... *that guarantees I'll never lose it.* So I parody that quote and adapt it to my beliefs:

"What good is it for man to get to know everything if he doesn't know self and his fellow man?"

The prevalent cultural current was to motivate people towards the acquisition of knowledge, especially maths, science and languages. With time it ended up becoming a high society passport. We saw waves of pedantry or a kind of affectation in one's way of speaking and writing. There was -and still is to a certain extent- a certain snobbery about knowledge in general. Even to this date, one is still looked at as less than competent if he doesn't have a grade 12 education which, for me, means nothing.

A grade 12 education opens certain doors for some A and B students in the pursuit of a higher education, but by no means guarantees success or happiness. And it says nothing about the individual's potential. Look at Jesus. As far as we know, he didn't even know his multiplication tables or how to spell cat… I'm surprised our culture isn't calling him "retarded!" In our modern society, *he wouldn't qualify for the job of garbage collector…*

That cultural inertia is common to every people on earth. In lots of ways, it's a combination of indoctrination and paralyzing insecurity. We find a trail used by the majority and we accept to follow it, in spite of the fact that, very often, it doesn't really suit us. But for the tranquility of mind and the false security it provides us with, we are ready to renounce to ever daring to follow our own star. Thus, never becoming all we can be or who we really are. In doing so, we betray ourselves.

In a word, we largely prostitute ourselves for a false security because of the fear of the unknown. It's also because –and mainly because- of the deformation that has been forced on us by our school's coercive straight jacket. We were taught to obey, to conform and to sacrifice our need of individualization *"for the benefit of the almighty establishment!"*

That's why it's so hard to engage people in something new like a school system in which we don't use our authority as a Damocles sword over the kids' heads for 12 years of their burgeoning life. That also explains why it took 7-8 years to implant a Quality School in Moncton, New Brunswick. That same socio-cultural inertia explains why man, after hundreds of thousands of years of evolution –or stagnation- has not yet learned to co-exist harmoniously with his brothers of the earth and still wars against them.

So, what am I saying? Would it be losing our time to try to change the culture in our society? As much as it will demand a lot of efforts on our part and that it will take some time, it can be done, a step at a time; we must apply love and understanding instead of coercion, cooperation and cohesion instead of competition.

"Habit is habit, and not to be flung out the window by man, but coaxed downstairs, a step at a time."

— Mark Twain (1835-1910)

The worst place where we could try to bring about some changes,-any changes- would be to expect the government to change. It won't happen until we, the citizen, change. The second worse place would be the church. Most are supposedly interested in humanities but in a cultish kind of way. Correct me if I'm wrong, but they all swear that they have **"The Truth"**... and that they are the only one to have it.

The third worse place is the school. The fact that our schools need so much improvement is not the principals, the teachers, or the parents, fault. They are victims of a political and capitalist way of looking at our children, first as a future asset for the industry and as an easy herd to manage as voters and soldiers. Finally, the most important place is the family.

Why the family? Let's dream for a moment and pretend that the government decides to fix the problem of compulsory schooling. First they pass a new law making school non compulsory. Surely some kids would stop going. I don't know how serious the exodus from school would be. I presume that, at the beginning, it might be quite significant. Eventually though, things would get back to **"abnormal."**(I nearly said to normal…)

The school would still be a concentration camp, but without *"the mental barb wires."* Now not willing to lose all the students and look bad, the teachers might improve their attitude with the students. They wouldn't afford to be disrespectful and bully them anymore, because the students could walk out in the middle of the teacher's sentence and give him **"the major finger salute."** The teachers who were coercion enthusiasts would probably lose lots of their students in their classes unless they change their approach. Most teachers don't know how, or don't trust another approach. They just know/trust the coercive approach and they would have just lost their whip if they didn't coerce…

Well, there's a good ending to that story. In 1993, William Glasser found the first "Quality School" in the world. It's still operating to this day in Huntingdon, Wyoming, U.S.A. and in many countries around the world.

Hundreds of thousands of people are aware of the existence of that new school system. Hundreds of thousands of people are aware that it's definitively a better school system than our archaic school system. Thousands of people have visited some of these schools and saw them in action with their own eyes. They have seen how much happier and more mature the students of these schools are. In spite of that, the population at large is not aware of its existence. But at the same time, they know *how much an egg Mc Muffin and a coffee cost at McDonald…*

I live in Langley, British Columbia. At about an hour from here, in North Vancouver, a Quality School is in the process of being implanted or could have received its certification lately. I personally know the William Glasser counselor who managed its implementation. Her name is Lucy Scott and I took the William Glasser's basic and advanced training courses from her. She's a very good counselor and I really enjoyed learning under her guidance. It has dramatically changed my outlook on life.

How many people in Vancouver are aware that there's a Quality School in North Vancouver? Do they know what it means for the future of the kids who are attending now and of those who will attend that school in the future? I feel generous today. I'll say 10 to 15 percent, and it has been started around 20 years ago. They just have to cross a bridge and they are in North Vancouver… Now, what about North Vancouver people? How many know about that school and its incredible advantage over the regular school for their kids? Could it be as high as 50%? And why is there only one Quality School? Why isn't there any other similar school in the process of being implemented? It doesn't cost more to operate and the government doesn't oppose them.

So where's the problem? The problem is us the people.

We suffer from a paralyzing condition called socio-cultural inertia! Most people in North Vancouver who heard about the Quality School in their city probably think that it's one of these new age gimmicks. Without blinking they probably judged it not worth losing their time and their spit looking into it.

CHAPTER 14

Humanization 101 at work

"The task of the modern era was the realization and humanization of God – the transformation and dissolution of theology into anthropology."

— Ludwig Feuerbach

At the beginning of the month, I read an article in The Province, a very popular daily newspaper in our province. That article talked about the school board in a neighbouring city, planning to distribute bibles to 5th grade students whose parents agreed with that practice. The B.C. Humanists Association, led by Ian Bushfield believes that we shouldn't see proselytizing in classrooms.

This article written by Jennifer Saltman reads :

"A group of B.C. atheists is asking the Abbotsford School District to stop distributing religious material- including biblical texts supplied by the Gideons- to students in its public schools."

Ian Bushfield, executive director of the B.C. Humanist Association said *"the association is holding off any further action until it receives a response from the Abbotsford School District.*

However, if the district fails to change its policy, the association will attempt to have an atheist comic book distributed to students. If that request is denied, there could be a legal challenge based on the Canadian Charter of Rights and Freedoms."

A parent, Tara Macrae, added: *"We don't hand out copies of the Qur'an, we don't hand out copies of any other religious material."*

Romeo Gauvreau, B.A.,

"If I decided to bring that article to your attention, it's because I see it as an example of how we the people can get involved in the cultural tsunami and have our voice heard. And if needed be, to take action to change what we see as an attempt at the indoctrination of innocent children. These are threatened to be brainwashed with mumbo jumbo material filled with unproven legends, or plain and simple gloomy fairy tales. The public school system already indoctrinates them far beyond reason or sanity."

"I congratulate Ian Bushfield, executive director of the B.C. Humanist Association *and the* B.C. Humanist Association *for their valued intervention and the smart way they plan to push the envelope by distributing an atheist comic book to the students. It's a non-aggressive and a safe intervention, respectful of the students and of the population. It's an example of humanization in action."*

"Religion is based . . . mainly on fear . . . fear of the mysterious, fear of defeat, fear of death. Fear is the parent of cruelty, and therefore it is no wonder if cruelty and religion have gone hand in hand. . . . My own view on religion is that of Lucretius. I regard it as a disease born of fear and as a source of untold misery to the human race."

— Bertrand Russell

The dehumanization of women

Which one of these two institutions has done more to subjugate women: culture or religion? It's probably culture since religions probably came a bit later than culture. But religion didn't lose any time to reinforce the subjugation of women. The bible talks about women as the source of all evil on earth.

"Sin began..." with a *"woman..."*, and thanks to *her we must all die*.

Ecclesiasticus / Sirach - Chapter 25

How could someone say such a stupid statement and attribute it to God? And there's more:

"The women should keep silent in the churches. For they are not permitted to speak, but should be in submission, as the Law also says. If there is anything they desire to learn, let them ask their husbands at home. For it is shameful for a woman to speak in church."

1 Corinthians 14:34-35

I don't mind certain groups of people having a cult like the Catholics have, if it entertains them. But to go as far as saying such stupidities and injustices is pushing the envelope too far. For me, religions that push their version of the bible on populations should be sued for spiritual abuse. Especially when it's done to children that are there against their will, prisoners of the school and not having the maturity to see the gibberish nature of the material imposed on their young minds. That is child abuse of the worst kind and should not be imposed by schools or tolerated by humanists.

CHAPTER 15

The Establishment

"A man's ethical behavior should be based effectually on sympathy, education, and social ties and needs; no religious basis is necessary. Man would indeed be in a poor way if he had to be restrained by fear of punishment and hope of reward after death."

— *Albert Einstein*

I do not deny the need for the establishment... At least it allows us to identify the most power hungry and egotistical individuals among us that otherwise might be difficult to single out and steer clear from... The establishment contains the highest concentration of sociopaths of our society. It's like if they were attending a conference for psychos which keeps them in view. This way, it's safer for us and easier to target for our rubbish removal program...

And if by any chance I hurt somebody's feelings among them, he should resign. His curriculum vitae is lacking an important requirement for him to be part of the establishment. I mean that thing about having feelings...He doesn't fit the criteria of his function...

"There's a plot in this country to enslave every man, woman, and child. Before I leave this high and noble office, I intend to expose this plot."

President John F. Kennedy 7 days before his assassination.

Did he get killed because of what he said that day? I

doubt it. The plan to kill him had been on the back burner for a long time before that day. They killed him because he was the type of man that would say things like that. There was also the fact that he supposedly had slept with Marilyn Monroe, and, with the vapors of alcohol helping to loosen his tongue …and tightening his manhood, he might have talked too much.

We will never know for sure why President Johnson would have had him killed- if he did- but:

Jackie Kennedy "believed LBJ had her husband killed according to tapes. "Jackie Kennedy" believed Lyndon B. Johnson was behind the 1963 assassination of her husband President John F. Kennedy.

*www.irishcentral.com › News*Feb 15, 2016

On the other hand, the CIA *did not* like President Kennedy. I believe that he was a smart man and a good man. That probably did him in.

Closer to us, in our beautiful country, Canada, we don't have a president. But we have the equivalent and we call him Prime Minister. I'm not sure that the word *"prime"* is appropriate here… Because they're not first in anything. All they will do has been done before. A new Prime Minister means a new face but not much else. They're not allowed to tamper with the *status quo.* They must continue to do *the usual brown nosing the corporations are used to.*

Anthony J. D'Angelo tells us that *''the people who oppose your ideas the most are those who represent the establishment that your ideas will upset".*

Both the family and the school try their best to have their children fit in society. The problem is that not every part of society is beneficial to our children. They have to follow the law, but they don't have to agree with all of them or to like them. They should see it for what it is and not let it contaminate their mind with its pernicious propaganda.

Here's a bumper masters" sticker I'd like to see...

"We are the proud parents of a child who has resisted his teachers' attempts to break his spirit and bend him to the will of his corporate masters."

"George Carlin"

I taught school for 6 years at the secondary level. As you know, in the front row of each class, we can see the "A" students. They're very attentive; they take notes and swallow every word that comes out of your mouth. Teachers love them. They never cause any discipline problems and are easy to manage.

To tell you the truth, I was a weird teacher. I felt bothered by them. I felt sorry that they swallowed every word from every teacher. I felt sorry for them because they were like putty in the hands of a potter. *They had their built-in bullshit detectors in the off position or probably not installed yet.* They were being modified, re-shaped and enslaved. They were prostituting themselves for marks on a sheet of paper, to please their parents and the teachers who pressured them into betraying who they were in order to fit in our alienated society and thus, please them and the teachers and submit to the establishment.

I didn't like them to try and make me part of their *betraying whom they really were, in order to please others.* That prostitution, to me, is far more destructive than that of the sex trade workers. I don't judge the women who sell their sexual services to men for money.

If they do a good job at helping men achieve climax, they are honest and acceptable to me. However, men are not always fair in their judgment of these women. Also they're not always humane with them. Some mistreat them and brutalize them and even steal back the money they paid plus the money these women had from work with previous clients. If the Johns were as honest as these girls are, I would encourage the sex trade. They need support and protection from society. They are human beings doing an important job and doing it well. I met and chat with a few young sex trade workers and I never look down on them.

The last one, in Vancouver, 20 years ago, told me horrifying stories of what she had experienced. I had picked her up as she was hitchhiking on her way to work. We had a chat that was interesting and educating for me. I'm very sympathetic to them, without having ever used their services.

Coming back to those "A" students, I remember one day saying to one who was particularly looking at me as one looks at God and telling her: *"If you don't do something wrong soon, I'll have to reprimand you!* I probably said it in a more polite way, but it meant exactly that.

The establishment is only strong of our weakness. They put us in little cubicles that restrain our movements, social and political movements, that is, and we comply. We bitch, but to the wrong person. You to me, me to you, and at the wrong time: a day after the elections!

Many books, I'm sure, have been written about -and against- the establishment and many more will be. It's one of those subjects that we cannot ignore since we're victims of it every day, every moment of our life. It's like a cloud always there and hiding the sunlight from us. Until we sensitize ourselves and others to its corrosive effects and re-conquer our birthright to freedom, we'll continue barking at the moon with the results we know. But understand me well. I'm not endorsing violence ...except to do violence to ourselves.

"The law will never make a man free; it is men who have got to make the law free."

— Henry David Thoreau

Twilight

The day is already consumed,
The sun declining far away,
On golden sea its day resumed,
The horizon out of the way.

Like the soul of a moribund
That retires in the silence,
Its gently shades of red abound,
On golden sea slowly balances.

Pure gold water seems to swallow
The silent sinking great Monarch
Without a sound the scene mellows,
The whole nature plunged in the dark.

And like the end of the outcome,
Of this drama for mother Earth,
Like a curtain down the night comes,
Thus hiding the sight of the Hearth.

Roméo Gauvreau, Feb. 15, 1959,
Translated from French Feb. 15, 2013.

CHAPTER 16

Is Desindoctrination a utopia?

"Tell people there's an invisible man in the sky who created the universe, and the vast majority will believe you. Tell them the paint is wet, and they have to touch it to be sure."

— George Carlin

If I check on Google, I find this definition of utopia: *an imagined place or state of things in which everything is perfect.* There's no saying that humanity would be perfect if we succeeded in eliminating indoctrination. Elimination might be utopist; reduction is not.

What the quote above is telling me, is that people check the paint because they feel they cannot trust others ... anymore. They have been lied to by just about everybody that had authority in their lives: their parents, their teachers, their priests or pastors, the political and judicial system etc. They have been betrayed, coerced, threatened, punished, belittled, abused, violated and the list continues. In spite of that, the people they should trust continue to control them with the whip of the fear of God, the fear of their parents, the fear of the principal, the fear of the cops, the fear of the judge, the fear of the government and *the fear ...of fear!*

If and when more people realize that most religions are based on fairy tales, most of them on *scary* fairy tales, there's a good chance that, the fear diminishing, the right to think for themselves will become more appealing than ever before. They will then give themselves the right to voice their opinions. It will not happen overnight and not without serious socio-cultural frictions!

It would not have happened if, but for the advent of the proliferation of computers and most particularly because of the explosion of communications brought about by Facebook, Twitter, and the smart phones proliferation in all the advance countries …and others.

The new generation is 99% addicted to the smart phone and spend a large portion of its waking hours *glued to it.* I don't have to expand too much on this point. If you got out of your house at least ten times in the last year, chances are you saw people holding these gadgets in their hands eleven times out of ten! That's how widespread it is.

I believe that a lot of people, especially the older people, are worried about what will become of our youth. They're even worried about what is happening to the world! They are incensed by those who text while driving. Or by the mothers who are constantly playing on their gadget while breastfeeding their baby. What about the risk of the harmful electromagnetic waves for the baby? Or what is very common, sitting in a restaurant with 2 or 3 friends and all of them talking to other people, *other* than the people they're with!

To lots of us, it doesn't make sense. We see it as very impolite for them to play on their gadgets while sitting with their friends. What's up with that?

Well, I'll give you my opinion of that phenomenon that is surging all over the world like ***"an epidemic of acute madness."***

CHAPTER 17

The Babel Tower... or the Revolutionary Cell Phones

"Education should not be about building more schools and maintaining a system that dates back to the Industrial Revolution. We can achieve so much more, at unmatched scale with software and interactive learning."

— Naveen Jain

...that phenomenon that is surging all over the world like an epidemic of acute madness. For the academia, it's not a way to start a sentence. For me, pleasing the academia comes pretty low on my list of priorities, as you must know by now. If I repeated that part of the sentence, it was to make sure that we're all on the same page. Of course, I don't believe that what we're seeing with the cell phone revolution is a sign of acute madness.

Without being able to analyze the phenomenon like maybe a smart sociologist would, I believe that it might be too early to decree that the new generation is sick and that the world is going to the dump *the pedal to the metal.* It is possible, however, that that last statement could be true. I think it's too early to rule on what is happening in the world ...and to the world. Something is happening and it's happening extremely fast, if we talk about a changing world. That is a revolution of greater amplitude than any revolution we ever saw or heard about in the history of mankind.

That statement might surprise a lot of my readers and I

understand. Five years ago, I wrote a book in French which I didn't publish yet. In order to write that book called: *Les cellulaires revolutionaires,* which I translate by *The Revolutionary Cell Phones*, I had to put a lot of thinking and research into the subject. I see why lots of people are not impressed by the phenomenon. Like me, they don't quite understand it and many look down on it as a stupid fad. I believe it's not a fad and it's not stupid. Here's what I think about the nature and the implications of that phenomenon.

In the story about the Babel Tower, if I remember well, people tried to build a tower that would reach *''the heavens''*. These people were of one language and if they succeeded in reaching the heavens, nothing would be impossible to them. God seeing that, came down and confused them in their language. They abandoned the construction of the tower, not understanding each other anymore, and spread all over the world. So goes the legend.

I would be really curious to know what the real meaning of that legend is. I don't take the bible legends *verbatim*, but I believe that there was possibly a real event that happened and that it got adulterated in time with translations, additions, subtractions, interpretations etc. A few thousand years ago, when aliens visited the earth, as I and others believe, there were no words to explain the phenomenon and very likely, it got expunged from the literature of the time as being blasphemous or delusional in nature.

I do believe in UFOs for many reasons. In the last 60 years, I heard about many sightings by friends and family and, not wanting to be outdone, I saw one myself in 2002, in Nouvelle, Quebec. I was with a friend of mine, traveling by car, on the top of a mountain overlooking the village.

On my right, I noticed a powerful jet of light aiming down at the village at the foot of that mountain, on our left. WE stopped and observed it for a good 20 minutes, and seeing no movement or hearing no noise whatsoever, we continued on our trip to the restaurant. The next day, her brother came for lunch with us, and as soon as we started talking about the previous night vision, he got all excited. At the same time we had seen that strange jet of light hitting the village at about five miles from where we were, he was passing through that village and couldn't understand what he was seeing. It was around 8.30 at night and the village was all illuminated like if it was daytime.

Coming back to our cell phone hysteria, there are two main alternative futures I'm interested in. First, the young generation has been like dazzled by a magic gadget and they are hopelessly mesmerized or hypnotized by its capacity to make them forget about the world's cruelty, the world's apathy to the senseless violence of the wars, by the racism and the general dehumanization they're witnessing. It also, and maybe especially, helps them forget the unnatural life they're coerced into by the compulsory and wicked school system. The cell phone is a potent and addictive drug that allows them to forget 90% of the time that the Babel tower they dwell in is going to crumble at any moment. They cannot face that conjecture any longer …and I understand them.

The second possibility is that they are disconnecting from the world and disconnecting from their friends and only connect with a hundred or a thousand imaginary friends they never met and probably never will. They're seemingly giving up on the will to try and humanize the world. ("Seemingly" is the key word here.)They lost hope in mankind and don't see how they could do anything about it. Therefore they're negating the contact with the old generation, i.e. the people who don't worship the new god named Smart Phone.

Call me naïve if you want, but I don't believe that this second hypothesis is going to make the world crumble. On the contrary, here's what I believe will happen.

For a while, we might face a wave of disconnection of the young generation and eventually of the whole population, let's say in another 25-30 years; a disconnection of people with the inhumane 21st century reality! In other words, a kind of disconnecting from what is happening to the world around them.

I know I'm traveling in an imaginary world, here. But, according to Einstein:

"Imagination is more important than knowledge. For knowledge is limited to all we now know and understand, while imagination embraces the entire world, and all there ever will be to know and understand."

— Albert Einstein

Why do I believe that the present cell phone hysteria might not bring the world to the brink of disaster more than it is presently? There are a few reasons why I believe that, instead of being the beginning of the end, it has a chance of being a new start of the humanity towards a better world. That's what I would like to explore with you in the next chapter.

CHAPTER 18

Compulsive communicating

"Cell phone dependency is now called compulsive communicating. Chain dialers call continually to get another fix."

— Spokesman Review

Man has apparently set foot on the moon in 1969. It didn't impress me much. Man has landed a capsule on Mars in 2012. It impressed me even less! Why am I not impressed by those pseudo exploits? Humanity is drowning in wars and manipulations from the establishment, and we spend hundreds of billions of dollars to land on the moon and bring back a few rocks!!! Why not tell the world *the real reason* why Americans went to the moon? I'll be talking about that in a further chapter. According to Wikipedia, *"Facebook is a social networking service launched in February 2004, owned and operated by Facebook. It was founded by Mark Zuckerberg with his college roommates and fellow Harvard University student Eduardo Saverin."*

By the end of 2015 there were around 1.51 billion Facebook users worldwide. *That impresses me a lot!* Why would the invention of an app on a gadget impress me? Generally it doesn't. The Facebook phenomenon is different in many ways. Here's how.

Right or wrong, I believe that it might be the most important social or cultural event at the humanity level in the last 5 to 10 thousand years. One cannot have a normal productive life without learning how to establish a connection with self and with others. Man is a social animal.

Is it possible that what we look at as an insignificant gadget, the cell phone, would represent, at some level, the most sophisticated tool of connection of people around the world?

In another 5 years, there might be well over 2 billion people connected through Facebook. It will probably be the first time on earth that such a large number of people are in contact at any given time, 24/7. There are other apps like Twitter and Instagram who also connect people. Facebook and Twitter are the two most popular social networks in the world.

I'm sure some other apps, more sophisticates and more magics will appear in the next few years and possibly replace the two most popular apps of today. I seriously believe that unfathomable gadgets are already in the making in someone's mind and they might make us look back on what is the cat's meow now, as "passé". From multi-tasking to multi talking

"My cell phone is my best friend. It's my lifeline to the outside world."

— Carrie Underwood

How sad! I personally see two major problems with people becoming that dependant on a cell phone. If we put aside the desire to fit in, which is not a problem *per se,* we're left with a few serious tendencies. First, there's a strong narcissistic tendency. It says: **listen to me and look at me!** Second, it seems, it could be a possible form of escapism from the harsh reality of life.

Third, it has become kind of a rite of passage. You're not cool if you don't do it. And since they have been raised to conform and to follow the bleating mass on the most taken trail, they want to fit in at all cost.

And that, even if it's killing them one toke at a time, one binge drinking at a time, one fix at a time: ecstasy, meth, crack cocaine smoking, heroin snorting and a whole lot wider arsenal of lethal weapons of *masses destruction.*

Texting while driving

"It's easier for a rich man to ride that camel through the eye of a   needle directly into the Kingdom of Heaven, than for some of us to give up our cell phone."

— Vera Nazarian

With this new appendix to the human body the young generation subtracts itself from the real reality and moves in a virtual reality of sort. Intelligent love is a gift of life, part of the package deal. We're born with it. We can, over the years, learn how to become more skillful in how we use our tool kit, in the same manner as one can learn how to use an indented chisel for woodcarving.

The fact that one owns all the tools of the sculptor does not make him a qualified sculptor. No more than being gifted with a very strong intelligence makes us act intelligently, therefore lovingly. There's no other way to travel through a happy ever after life.

So why do they do it? I do not know the real reason, and I can only assume that they do it to escape the boredom of rush hour driving, of their work and of their lives …maybe!

It is a drug like any other drug, at their fingertips and it costs nothing ...except fines, sometimes, and damage to vehicles, when *it's not injuries or perfectly preventable deaths.*

And before we throw the stone to that person, we must remember that we are all irresponsible to different degrees. We must remember that the young generation has been catapulted in the future by the unprecedented evolution and proliferation of communications. I often say that *the only stupid animal in all of the creation is man.* It is also the wildest and most dangerous!

In 2010, distracted driving was a contributory factor in 104 fatal collisions in British Columbia (RCMP). (Translated in English by the author)

www.stps.on.ca/... / Distracted-Driving

If we look at somewhere else in Canada, we find much of the same.

TORONTO - *Are Ontarians getting the message on distracted driving?*

Ontario Provincial Police Sgt. Kerry Schmidt says his officers "continually see people driving while being distracted.

"In terms of 'Are they getting the message?' I think they know the rules, I think people are quite aware of the situation," Schmidt said. "But in terms of them thinking they're the problem, I think that's where the question is."

The trouble is, people think they can get away with

driving while doing something else, he said.

"They think they're able to multi-task and text and drive," Schmidt said. "It doesn't seem like they're getting the message all the time."

While the number of fatal crashes in Ontario has declined in recent years, statistics from the OPP released in February indicate distracted driving is one of the top four causes of fatal collisions in the province.

The OPP said inattentive driving, impaired driving, not wearing a seatbelt and speeding are the top four factors in crash deaths.

"We certainly do see distracted driving as one of the biggest causal factors for fatal collisions," Schmidt said.

By Maryam Shah, Toronto Sun

We were born in a century of dumbed down and subjugated human beings. Our youth was born in a century that is completely different from the one we were born in. I think our youth will not be as easy to enslave and to domesticate as we were -and still are- in most cases.

In travelling, we have passed from the bull to the jet, but them, they will pass from the jet to the interplanetary and possibly to the intergalactic travel. We're wasting our time and theirs if we think we can enslave them as we have been. They are probably not more intelligent than we are; but they don't think on the same wavelength as we do, thank God! Please don't be mistaken by what I'm saying. I'm not saying that they are better than we are and that they are going to accomplish miracles while facing the horrible future we have bequeathed them in inheritance.

What I'm saying is that humanity has been standing around for at least 15,000 years and did not move forward socially. We are as domesticated now as we were then and there will be no human evolution of our societies as long as we shall accept any indoctrination, from whatever source it might come. And I believe that the new generation, if life on earth does not go extinct in the next 50 years ...*or before*, will not be "indoctrinatable" and "domesticatable" in as high a degree as we were. But they might be more "democratisable" than we are.

The transition has begun with tiny details hardly perceptible to us. That societal revolution will not be brought about in one day nor in a century probably if it happens at all. They might throw everything in the air and maybe bring about horrible conditions in the world for a while. But we must remember that they have no model from which to be inspired by and they should especially *not be inspired by the accomplishments of previous generations or by history*! There is nothing there worth inspiring them!

CHAPTER 19

From trivial apps to lethal traps

"I'm old fashioned with my cell phone. I like that human contact and I think it's important."

— Giovanni Ribisi

The word apps is becoming part of our vocabulary. Everybody under 50 knows what it means. People over 50 and in my age group, a lot less... The abbreviated word means an *application* or *applications* in its plural form.

Google defines it as *a self-contained program or piece of software designed to fulfill a particular purpose; an application, especially as downloaded by a user to a mobile device.*

Lately, we hear a lot about a new form of bullying that didn't exist when most of us were in school: the vicious and relentless *cyber bullying*. Instead of being exposed to bullying mainly during recesses and between classes, on school days, victims are now harassed 24/7 on cyber space. The victims have no respite and nowhere to hide. It's an alarming situation.

I believe that strict laws calling for stiff penalties will be passed to try and curb that new trend. *It's a waste of time and money!* It will not stop the cyber bullying! Yes, we have to find these bullies ...and help them before some of their victims commit suicide out of desperation like Amanda Todd and numerous others.

In the case where young girls end up in trouble after being fooled by an adult sex offender, like in the case of the young girl from Coquitlam B.C. I just mentioned, the perpetrator was a 35 year old Dutch man, Aydin Coban, operating from the Netherlands. He was involved in 39 cases of child sexual exploitation and extortion. He is facing five charges in B.C.: extortion, internet luring, criminal harassment, possession and distribution of child pornography like in the Todd case. Because his case is ongoing in the Netherlands, Canada has not succeeded to extradite him yet in order for him to face charges here.

I think the vulnerability of our youth facing internet luring is not easy to fix. The internet luring *sickos* are expert at what they're doing and are extremely difficult to catch. So, you have an expert at conning people and the victim, in most cases, is an innocent young girl who is looking for a romantic relationship in the lion's den. The chance of getting a genuine relationship is not great. That young girl is going to school with hundreds of boys and she doesn't find any of them satisfying her requirements. Maybe that's where the problem is. Her idea of a romantic partner is either unrealistic or the young guys in her school are not behaving the way a normal teenager should.

Is it possible that young guys aged 14 to 17 are not as mature as they would be if the school hadn't dumb them down in the first place? Is it possible that women are less affected by the dumbing down effect of the school system than the boys are? In general, they tend to mature earlier than boys do. I don't know the answer, but I tend to believe that our male teenagers are definitely not as mature as they would be if they had received a normal education in real life, not indoctrination in that alienating concentration camps they called public schools!

Chapter 20

Bullying and cyber bullying

"Bullying is killing our kids. Being different is killing our kids and kids who are bullying are dying inside. WE have to save our kids whether they are bullied or they are bullying. They are all in pain."

— Cat Cora

I fail to see what right our society has to tell bullies to stop bullying! Really! When it comes to bullying, some parents do it. Some students do it to other students. Some teachers do it to some students and to some other people including teachers. Our governments consistently coerce us. If you want an example of it, just join a protestation movement and assemble in the street and see how long it will take before the police come up with a variety of very unpleasant means to have you get back in your hole with the other cockroaches and to shut up! During the spring of 2012, in Montréal, Quebec, we saw a perfect example of it.

The government having announced its intention of raising the university tuition fees, the students' union organized a protest and they gathered in the street. Then, I ask myself the question: "What harm would have it done, for the government to invite and meet their union representatives to discuss the students' concerns and the government's financial situation?" These were all university students, all smart kids. Why did they have to go and protest in the street in the first place? These are not criminals...Why not treat them with respect and dignity?

Through a meeting, they would have had the chance to debate their point of view with the government and possibly come to an agreement. Whatever the outcome of the meeting, they could have come out of it with their head held high and the principles of democracy would have been copiously reinforced.

Instead, the government passed the bill 78, which basically removes the right to protest from the citizens. That law requires that all protestations must be preceded by an 8 hours warning to the city, be composed of less than 50 people and that the exact location and itinerary of the protestation be given in advance ...and a few other emasculating rules like that! The government in power treats us...like we treat our kids in school: coercion, lack of respect, bullying and the rest. Back to school bullies and bullying.

Bullying is not a recent problem in schools. I personally experienced it as a witness and as a victim, while in seminary (college) from 1950 to 1957. I stayed in that seminary till 1959. Why did I not suffer from bullying for the last two years? It just happened that in 57-58, I grew from 5ft 7 to 6 ft, weighing 195 pounds of muscles... They though better than to continue and try to push me around!

I believe that there was a lot less of it then, than there is since the gradual apparition of the cyber gadgets.

I believe men have bullied certain other men and probably most women since the beginning of time. Countries have bullied other countries and are still doing it as you read this book. One just has to watch the news at night to see and hear about wars, be it countries against countries or civil wars, tearing and decimating the population like we have in Syria at the moment; by April 2016, it's estimated that there have been around 400,000 deaths, *and counting!*

Having said that, I'm totally against bullying against countries, against women or against any citizen, bullies included. In school, amongst possible causes of bullying, we must consider the high level of boredom causing frustration and aggressiveness among certain students, more than among others. Students who are victims of coercion at home, on top of the constant coercion in school, are much more prone to bully others.

If we refer to Wikipedia, we find this definition of bullying:

"Bullying is the use of force. Behaviors used to assert such domination can include verbal harassment or threat, physical assault or coercion, and such acts may be directed repeatedly towards particular targets."

And further, it adds:*"...the use of force, threat, coercion to abuse, intimidates, or aggressively imposes domination over others*,"

If we believe this part of the quote, the coercive attitude of our school system itself is a form of bullying!

The bullying phenomenon should stop us dead in our tracks! *"It's a red flag society can't afford to ignore!"* We're witnessing a reaction to coercion that is extremely serious and distressing… We shouldn't throw the book at those kids; I want to take them aside and hug them, instead! I believe some of their parents, their school and society as a whole, have let them down. Their reaction in that manner is a cry for help. They are drowning in the stormy seas of the all-engulfing coercion. They need help! If we don't take the time to help them get their life back on track, they will probably waste their life away.

They should be pulled out of school and sent for psychological assessments and treatments or, at least, to a coercion free Quality School, whenever possible. Counseling for them and their parents is a must. The psychological damage inflicted on some kids by the school, in most cases, and by the parents, in lots of cases, contributes to change the kid into a bully and is not the kids' fault.

If nothing is done to help that child towards recovery, he is facing a life of unhappiness at work and possibly of spousal and child abuse. Besides, among adults, nobody likes a bully!

"By their mid-thirties, 60% of people who bullied in grades 6 through 9 have at least one criminal conviction. ...they are also more likely to carry weapons than non-bullies and may develop antisocial personality disorder. »"

(tweenparenting.about.comParentingTweens)

Bullying has always existed. We find it at every level of society, including in most families, between parents, between parents and children, and between siblings. It's therefore not surprising to find it in school. Consequently, it's a good place where to start to educate them on how to establish a satisfactory relationship with self and others and therefore develop a good self-esteem. But it can only happen if we also work at eliminating coercion at the source: in the family (80-90%?), and in the school (99.99%?). I don't believe punishments or threats will help solve a problem that is gaining alarming proportions. In doing so, we only compound the problem.

The bully and the victim both need serious help if we want them to have a chance at a normal productive life. Here's a new bill attempting to deal mainly with bullying. On November 30, 2011, the Ontario Government introduced Bill 13, Accepting Schools Act, 2011 in the legislature.

New Anti-Bullying Laws Across Canada,

Yosie Saint-Cyr:

"The Act would amend the Education Act to create bullying awareness week in schools and provide instruction regarding issues of bullying and dealing with situations where bullying occurs."

Saint-Cyr continues on, adding a very important component to the Act:

"and if there is a promise to protect and counsel victims and perpetrators, while threatening legal consequences, we should be better able to deal with bullying as it happens, and hopefully to prevent violence from escalating."

Did I read that well?

"…while threatening legal consequences!!!"

The big guns had to be brandished! How could it be otherwise? Governments breed coercion!

If, as I believe, coercion at home and/or at school creates bullies, it would amount to adding insult to injury. If the threat of expulsion doesn't deter the bullies and they end up getting expulsed, what happens to these kids then? Where do they go, what do they do? The parents want their kids in school *even if only for the babysitting advantage of the school system...*

There's nothing the courts, the school or the parents can do that will solve the problem, except removing the source of the problem: coercion in school and at home. **Bullies are not the cause of the bullying problem.** They are a sample of the victims of systemic coercion, a category of victims who end up reacting that way, while trying to stay afloat emotionally.

I see but one solution and it will take a while before we see tangible results. Certain attitudes of some parents with their children will have to change. The spirit of teaching will have to change. The number one lesson to teach kids will have to be the respect of self and of others. And to make the learning of that lesson possible, everybody will have to join in the effort to respect themselves, others, and these kids, *always, and wherever they are.* In doing so, kids will learn to respect and love themselves. After that, everything is possible.

And as much as the pursuit of such a transformation might seem utopian, there is no greater pursuit of humanization than that one. When we reach that goal, we will see the flourishing of a true civilization possibly for the first time on earth. I'm aware that for certain people, I will come across as an idealist and a dreamer and that the pursuit of such a goal is an utopia. But nothing is further from the truth. *We overcame cannibalism, didn't we?*

Closer to us, the Quality School of Corning in the state of New York, has not only changed the school atmosphere but also that of the city of Corning. If only Quality Schools succeed in preventing the proliferation of bullies and bullied, it is well worth the effort of implementing them.

That it would be difficult to accomplish such a change in the foundation of our society and that it might take a few generations is definitively realistic. We must remember that raising children is the most difficult, but the most important job on earth. Nobody has ever said that man's evolution would be easy and fast and that the results were guaranteed.

But in working together toward such a goal, we help kids and ourselves grow in the process. And that's a big part of why we're here on this earth in the first place. Another part of the equation of bullying is the victim or the bullied. He is part of the problem in some cases. He is often a person whose spirit has been broken, often at home, and somehow he attracts abuse to himself by his negative attitude showing his vulnerability. When teased, he doesn't react in the proper way. He doesn't know how. He needs help before he himself starts bullying smaller kids in a compensatory or reactive kind of way.

As for people who could help him and the bully, let's hope they will see the light and not attempt to control the bullying by bullying the bullies. The situation will improve, in time, but first the social inertia has to be tackled in order to accomplish any change to our institutions. There would be a lot more to say about the bullying. A whole book wouldn't be enough to cover the subject properly.

"The culture of bullying includes daily activities and the way people relate to each other. A bullying culture emphasizes a win/lose way of thinking. It also encourages domination and aggression."

Wikipedia

Talking about our win/lose way of thinking, one just has to look at our national sport, which is not the worst in that domain, to understand how much useless violence is still involved in that sport. I say still because it has improved in the last 20-30 years. In those days, if they would have removed all violence from hockey, the arenas would have been half empty.

Sports like boxing and kick boxing are barbarian and primitive. There's a percentage of the population who enjoys seeing people being massacred. It's like a reminder of the old sport of the Christians thrown in the lion's dens…

Those people possibly use projection to remedy their inhibitions. It's kind of a revenge for the ills that bequeathed them on the bumpy roads of their life.

CHAPTER 21

A new world order?

"If the United Nations once admits that international disputes can be settled by using force, then we will have destroyed the foundation of the organization and our best hope of establishing a world order."

—Dwight D. Eisenhower

Before you assume that I believe in the philosophy of *the new world order* of the *Illuminati*, I really don't. There will definitely be major changes in the world order we now know as the world affairs. No doubt about it. Unless the world superpowers get into a destructive war like a nuclear war or worse, which is possible, life on earth as we know it is over, done with. I believe that either we'll blow the world apart or we'll humanize it!

Different from the Illuminati club for the rich and powerful, the *illuminated* brotherhood is, on the other hand, for everybody who realizes that what is, is not what could and should be. What could and should be is a lot better than the *status quo.* The generations of tomorrow will refuse to be indoctrinated by any organization, religious or other. And that includes school and government.

There's a possibility that I'm dreaming and completely out to lunch. I'm aware that when one tries to extrapolate and venture into unknown territories, one risks making a fool of himself. That's a risk that I'm ready to take. The picture we foresee of the reality of 2050 is not full of hope or encouraging. It reminds me of a boat on the Niagara River nearing the falls and the captain is in his cabin playing poker with his friends and only looking outside from time to time. And, before I forget, they're all having a drink.

They're roughly at a few hundred meters from the falls themselves. Anything can happen. The captain might decide to steer towards the shore and anchor for the night. There's a large gamut of possibilities; for an outsider, it looks pretty bad. Chances are they are doomed. We, as the world, are also on a course with destiny and it also looks pretty bad.

The new generations might react as the bystanders witnessing the boat going towards its demise and decide to gamble about where they're going and play their hand in a way never seen before: distancing themselves from the worldly big boat and take a chance on a new approach. That new approach consists of putting self ahead of the society's "captains" and swim to shore. By that, I mean following their instinct and the advice of their mind and of their heart instead of following our *partying leaders...* We have followed leaders since the dawn of time and look where it has left us: on our way to the realization of the Niagara falls *syllogism*.

One way or the other, we're going to face a certain type of new world order because we're on a collision course with ourselves. I think we're getting fed up with the way things are going and with the abuse we have submitted ourselves to since ...ever. We have had enough. We might be accused of being narcissistic or navel gazers. Would it be so bad if for a while, we had a generation of pacific *navel gazers trying to find their bearings? I think we have done worse through history than gazing at our navel ...or at* someone else's, *for that matter.*

Chapter 22

My brother's keeper

"If we desire a society in which men are brothers, then we must act towards one another with brotherhood. If we can build such a society, then we would have achieved the ultimate goal of human freedom."

— Bayard Rustin

I chose that title because I want to entertain you at the same time that I want to offer you some food for thought … if you feel hungry for it. I want to share with you the meaning of the brotherhood concept I believe in: two people in relationship with each other like two brothers. To achieve a satisfying relationship with someone else and for it to be pleasant and heartwarming for both, there's a prerequisite.

To really relate in a satisfactory manner with someone else, you must first have established a satisfactory relationship with yourself. It's a *"sine qua non"* condition to any relationship between two people. To love someone else in a fashion that is satisfactory to both, you must first learn who you are and love yourself, before you can love someone else.

The Greeks knew that, thousands of years ago. They had inscribed: *"knowti seauton!"* in the forecourt of the Temple of Apollo at Delphi. The Greek words mean *"know thyself"* and demonstrate that they were very advanced in humanization, in order to understand what we don't yet seem to understand in our world of advanced technology and materialism.

"We live in a world that has narrowed into a neighborhood before it has broadened into a brotherhood."

— Lyndon B. Johnson

From now on if the people would put as most important knowledge, not the knowledge of God, but the knowledge of self, we would be a whole lot better off for it! Not that there is a problem with knowing God. It is utterly impossible to know God if you don't know self. When you don't know self, you know nothing. And what is worse, you don't know that you know nothing. You don't know others, and you have no means of knowing them until you know self.

It might sound selfish or simplistic to some of you, but it would be selfish not to start there. So find out who and what you are. You're already very knowledgeable. Then proceed to learn how to love yourself. From then on, you have succeeded in life. The rest will consist of enjoying self and others and it will come naturally.

CHAPTER 23

Nonconformists

"The hope of a secure and livable world lies with disciplined nonconformists who are dedicated to justice, peace and brotherhood."

— Martin Luther King, Jr.

It sounds very good on paper, but how do we become disciplined nonconformists in real life? I have mentioned in the preface that I'm a nonconformist. I don't have any merit for being that way. I believe it's part upbringing at home and part choices we make in life, in spite of the fact that it's not popular in an indoctrinated population.

I must tell you that for reasons I don't understand, I have been a nonconformist for as long as I can remember. In 1960, I dumped my courses in Pedagogy because of my conviction that the curriculum of that university was not pertinent to education and was not helping the teacher in me to learn how to co-parent kids. I quit …and never regretted it.

My second really consequential nonconformist move was my dumping my religion (catholic) in 1962-63. One Sunday, during the sermon at mass, I was ready to get up in the church and give a piece of my mind to the preacher.

My wife, aware of my feelings at their boiling point, took my arm and said: *'I think we better go!"*

She was right. I could not continue to pretend that

everything was rosy. I'm not against a bordello selling sex, but I'm adamantly against a religion forcing you to prostitute yourself, and, in the process, having you pay them...for screwing you up!

The third time was when I started teaching and realized that the school system, far from having evolved since my school years, had become a governmental concentration camp of sort. The atmosphere had become more and more impersonal. Students were like numbers lost in a sea of bodies looking for their next classroom like cows looking for their stall in a barn.

The higher the density of a population, the more stressing it becomes for people. When a certain space is not provided around humans –like with any other animal- it creates a certain stress and can even arouse aggressiveness. But let us not jump ahead of ourselves...

Indoctrinated and nonconformist are at the opposite end of the spectrum. You cannot be nonconformist and still be indoctrinated or a sucker towards the establishment. Nonconformist has an undertone of revolutionary. That's where the word disciplined in *disciplined nonconformists* makes its triumphant entrance.

To be nonconformist could open the door to serious abuses. It's kind of being an anarchist and an asocial individual. It's not a humanist way of being. On the other hand, if you're a disciplined nonconformist, you will try to bring changes to the world, but in a pacifist and gentle way. Revolutions are generally violent and turn into a type of war some people call necessary and just. They never really contribute to advance civilization.

A disciplined nonconformist tries, instead, to change the world one person at a time, starting with self. It takes a long time but we have to remember that it took thousands of years for humanity to get to the point where we are at now. Inertia is a very strong law in physics and a very strong way of being in society. If it was easy to convert people to nonconformism, to humanism, this book would not have a reason for being...

Is it realistic to try and improve society and thus advance civilization and humanize life on earth? I like to think so. There's no hurt in trying and, in the meantime, one gets the feeling that he's fulfilling the goal, the challenge he has chosen to pursue. Why bother if it's so hard and quasi impossible? Why not let the world go by and do its thing? You could enjoy life and forget about the rest of the gang. If they end up destroying the world, so what?

I think it's a matter of conscience and integrity to want to improve your life and that of others. If one feels part of a brotherhood, it's normal that he would like to make other people happy or happier. We cannot change others, but if we improve life conditions on earth, in our corner of the country, others will benefit of it and possibly be happier. Is there any bigger and more useful challenge in life? I think it boils down to a choice of ideals and love of self and of "*thy neighbour*".

I think it's going to be a pretty good book, but people don't want to hear about *"good books"*. Here's what I mean. I'm a nonconformist ...to the hilt. I'll give you an example. I sometime say to people, when talking about child rearing, that one of the worst things that happen to us in life is to be raised by well-intentioned parents. It just sounds dumb to say such a thing. But when they ask me how I could say something like that, I explain what I mean in this manner.

As a rule, us parents don't know how to raise kids. Why do we not know? Because our parents copied their parents' methods, which parents didn't have a clue how to raise kids themselves. Why is it that animals know how to raise their offspring perfectly and we don't? I think that if mothers were left alone, not indoctrinated, not subjugated or alienated by men and society in general, they could raise their kids the right way, and that, without any help from anybody telling them what to do or what not to do.

Now let's suppose for a moment that that premise is right. There are two parts to my hypothesis. First, parents don't do a good job at raising kids because they don't seem to know how. Second, mothers have a nurturing instinct to raise kids the right way, without exterior help, if they're left alone.

Women would like to hear the second part of my hypothesis, but "parents" don't want to hear the first part of my hypothesis. They won't accept that somebody questions their way of raising kids. Do I think I know how to raise kids? No! I didn't do as well as I wish I could have done. I was not a "good parent" according to my criteria. The best thing I did for my kids was to never pronounce the words religion or God in their presence. If there is a God, -and I think there is- I trust that they will find Him by looking at the creation. And if they don't find Him in creation or in creatures around them, either God is not evident or there's no God ...or they're too dumb to recognize Him. Either way, my babblings are useless in that matter. They're certainly not as eloquent as the creation itself.

When Galileo said that the earth was round and turns

around the sun, they nearly killed him. People prefer to follow the gang on the comforting wide path, than to look for the truth on the narrow uncomfortable path. People want to be told, when the world is going to the dump, that God will come and save them. What I tell them is this: God will not come and save us from a disaster we have created while we have the means to avoid it, if only we would try. And what are those means? *"Do unto your fellowman as he would like done unto himself!"* Or *"treat people like good dog owners treat their dog ...and the world will be saved!*

I really believe that last sentence. Until then, we'll continue going to the dump *...the pedal to the metal.* How's that for a cheerful thought? Sorry, but that's who I am. I prefer rough truth than velvet lies. Al Gore calls it: *"the inconvenient truth."*

CHAPTER 24
Prerequisites of happiness

"Happiness is not something readymade. It comes from your own actions."

— Dalai Lama

I believe that we should try to teach that to our kids before we teach them about the birds and the bees, which should be taught around the age of 6 or 7 or whenever they're curious about it. The curiosity of children is something we take for granted and mostly a subject of conversation. We're amazed by it but too often we forget to realize that it is a very important tool for success and happiness.

We must be very careful not to tamper with -or discourage- their curiosity. It's there to assure their success at learning about themselves, others and the world around them. Be attentive to their questions and don't try to answer them in the order you believe preferable to the natural order the kids ask them.

His mind is pedaling as fast as it can and knows what questions to ask. A lot of the kids' questions sometimes seem senseless to adults. They're not senseless to them. An infant is a complete book of anthropology. Have the patience and the respect to read it as the pages turn for you at their proper rhythm.

When we're young and have our children, we're most of the time ignorant of the basics in life: to know ourselves. If we don't know ourselves we cannot know others. It might sound repetitive and it is. But I will never say it too much: "*knowti seauton!*" It's the alpha and the omega of any knowledge. Seems too simple?

I believe I am smart, but not smart enough to be the only one who discovered that precious principle. If you read the book by William Glasser called: *Choice Theory, A New Psychology of Personal Freedom*, you will realize a few things.

The first thing you should realize is how important is the way you relate to others. You will also realize that happiness depends on your skill at making certain enlightened choices. One of these choices is of not using coercion in your relationships with others, whatever their attitude towards you. The choices offered to you could be to distance yourself from them if their attitude is aggressive and disrespectful. Their attitude doesn't have to become your problem. You should not try to control their behaviour. The only behaviour you can control is yours. No ifs or buts ... "*The only behaviour you can control is yours!*" (William Glasser)

We have been taught to try to sway people into being civilized with us; it's a waste of time. I certainly can't explain his whole theory in a few lines. But if you're curious, I recommend this book, *before any other books in the world*, for anybody. Last year, I couldn't find that book among my stuff, so I order a new one and in the next six months ...are you ready? I read it not once, not twice, but *five* times!

You read that well. I read it five times and I will read it at least once for every year of the rest of my life. That book, to me, is a must for everybody, especially every parent and spouse. If I was sent into exile on a deserted island and could only bring one author, I would have zero hesitation: "William Glasser it is!"

And to give you an idea of what kind of humanist he was, he is selling this book at a price everybody can afford. Are you ready? I bought it last spring not for $20.00, not for $10.00, not for $1.00; *I paid one cent* and you can also have it for the same price, both new and used. I just checked amazon.com about the price, last week, since I'm buying it for a friend of mine. And believe me, Glasser could sell it for a lot more, even the used ones. I believe he wants people to read it and thus help his brothers and sisters of the world. I know of him very well for having taken courses from the William Glasser Institute, a few years ago, with Lucy Scott as instructor/counselor.

Too often, we look for happiness everywhere...where it's not. It's not in possessions, in prestige, in honors, in peoples' adulation or in position of power. None of those bring happiness. They might bring pleasure to some power hungry people, but pleasure is not happiness even if pleasure is an important component of happiness. The pleasure brought by happiness is not contingent on others or on circumstances. It's depending on you and you alone.

Only you can make yourself happy. Other people can do things that please you, procure some fun and pleasant moments for you. But they cannot control your behaviour or the way you feel. To be with the person that pleases you was your choice in the first place and can be over if and when you choose to. We choose to surround ourselves with the people who are compatible with our journey toward happiness instead of with the others. Those are things that most people know, but don't always proceed in that way.

The same thing goes with people who are unhappy. They see reasons why they're unhappy without going back to the root of the problem, which consist in the knowledge of self and love of self. It might seem too simplistic, but if you try it, you'll be surprised by what you'll find out.

"If you can laugh with somebody and relate to somebody, it becomes harder to dehumanize them. I think that most of what we are constantly bombarded with in terms of media leads you to a creation of "the Other" and a dehumanization of "the Other," and it's very much an us-versus-them conversation."

— Jehane Noujaim

Don't be a stranger

What chance was there of you and me meeting
On the same planet, the same century,
With the bad prospect of global warming,
This age of gadgets and of big hurry?

Against clock and time we run foolishly.
We run against time towards our death,
Like if we somehow were in a hurry
To meet Him ...or Her after our last breath!

Don't be a stranger when you meet me, please!
Like you, I've been taught to fear the unknown,
Men and animals, and pain and disease,
Original thoughts, new paths of our own...

Life is a challenge we don't understand,
Rushed by the strong wants we take for real needs,
The wants torture us and from where I stand,
The real needs are few, please listen and heed.

The fuel for our soul everywhere we look,
Like the air we breathe and the food we eat,
Been on every lips, said in every book,
And the more we give, the more we shall reap.

That fuel, so precious and so important,
We can't do without if we want to live,
If we want to grow through every instant,
To remain alert and remain alive.

That fuel we all have is the gift of love.
Everybody has to share it with others:
Without love from life or from the above,
Nothing makes sense, take my word, brothers

Roméo Gauvreau, decasyllabic, July 2013.

Conclusion

Like through a long pregnancy, I have been carrying this book in my heart and soul since 1968-69...

In the introduction, I was using that metaphor to explain the weight of carrying an ideal, a cause, something close to our heart like a mother does a baby... I have finally given birth to that book, after 48 years of that literary pregnancy. I had to share it with you because this way the weight is divided and shared. We hopefully are many sharing the content as a gift instead of as a burden. Happiness has to be warmly shared to maintain its freshness like fruits have to be refrigerated. Happiness doesn't survive in concealment. It grows in sharing, not in hogging.

I hope my book has entertained you for many long hours and, at the same time, has succeeded to provoke in you a reflection on our society, particularly on the family, the school, the church and the establishment with all it encompasses.

After we have informed the parents, implanted a humane school system and free people from indoctrination and coercion, we'll have a chance and the hope for a real humanistic evolution of our societies.

That can only happen by the recognition of the importance of stopping the coerced indoctrination of our kids at home, at school and at church. When with the best of intentions we mold kids so they fit in society, we perpetuate the "status quo" and the "status quo" is falling short of what we should be aiming at achieving as a society: self-actualization for our kids and a coercion free culture resulting in a democratic freedom that will accompany them for the rest of their life.

"It is no measure of health to be well adjusted to a profoundly sick society."

— Krishnamurti

Did I succeed to demonstrate that indoctrination impedes mind maturation? You be the judge. I hope I did. I like to leave my readers satisfied with my books.

Having given birth to this literary baby, my task is not over. I'll continue to help it grow and hopefully see to it that it continues to grow in your minds and consciousness. And that, to help bring about a new era in the pursuit of a culture that will continue the parent's mission of helping to actualize a new kind of citizen; a citizen with less *"show-offish"* knowledge, but more knowledge of self and of the other. I firmly believe that it's the real and only essential knowledge if we want the humanity to finally do a step forward in the right direction: *"the humanization of the world"*.

I owe you a heartfelt thank you for having accompanied me to the end. I never wrote a sentence without you in mind and the thought of how we were connecting.

Say brothers, say sisters,

"I love you, all of you!"

Your brother, Roméo

www.ingramcontent.com/pod-product-compliance
Lightning Source LLC
Chambersburg PA
CBHW030314130626
46549CB00002B/853